The Pacifica House

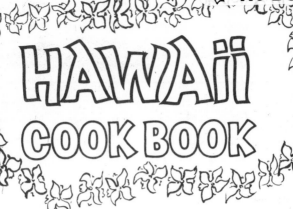

# HAWAii COOK BOOK

Edited by Don FitzGerald

Hawaiian Foods Consultant – Sybil Henderson

Introduction and History of
Hawaiian Foods by Erma Meeks Boyen
(Former Director of Home Economics,
Hawaiian Electric Co., Ltd., Honolulu)

Book Design by Liz FitzGerald

PACIFICA HOUSE, INC.   PUBLISHERS

# Mahalo Nui

# (Acknowledgments)

The Editorial Staff and Publishers of the Pacifica House HAWAII Cook Book wish to thank the following organizations for their assistance in producing this book: Department of Planning and Economic Development of the State of Hawaii, Hawaii Visitors Bureau, Fruit Shippers of Hawaii, Watercress of Hawaii, Inc., Spencecliff Corporation, Hawaiian Jam and Jelly Association, Hawaii Macadamia Producers Association, Hawaiian Electric Company, Waikikian Hotel, Kaaawa Farms, Coco Palms, Waiohai Hotel, Matson Navigation Company, Pan American World Airways, Hilo Chamber of Commerce.

Food Photographs co-ordinated — arranged by Henderson Associates.

The Pacifica House HAWAII COOK BOOK
by Don FitzGerald

Standard Book Number  911098-00-3
Library of Congress Catalog Card Number 65-4365
Produced and Printed in the United States of America
Copyright © 1965 by Pacifica House, Inc., Publishers

Published by
PACIFICA HOUSE INC., Publishers
P.O. Box 2131, Toluca Lake, California 91602, USA

# CONTENTS

# Introduction To Hawaii ...
# A Way Of Life

Hawaii . . . the Paradise of the Pacific! Yes, Nature has bestowed upon this chain of islands which lies anchored in the great Pacific, beauties which make it a "bit of heaven on earth". Surrounded by jade-blue waters rich in piscatorial bounty, cooled by the almost ever-present trade winds, nurtured by rains ranging from a feathery mist to a tropical downpour, blessed with awe-inspiring and fertile mountains and valleys, these entrancing islands are further enhanced by the blossoms of thousands of exotic flowers which in their gorgeous colors seem to reflect the magic of the frequent rainbows and the gorgeous sunsets.

Time and progress brought many peoples to the island shores. They liked what they saw and many of them stayed. Working together in the closeness of island life, each new group developed and shared its cultures and customs until now, hundreds of years later, Hawaii has emerged with a way of life which is bound to enrich all those privileged to either visit or to live within its sea-swept boundaries. You, too, can make Hawaii your way of life.

*Luau guests learn finger method of eating poi from Hawaiian hostess at right. A Luau meal is served traditionally on the ground or very low table which has been decorated with tapa cloth, grass mats, fresh fruits and an abundance of tropical flowers.*

# History Of Hawaiian Foods

Hawaii is "paradise unlimited" for the gourmet. A brief review of Hawaii's history will help us to understand how these far-flung islands gained this reputation. The islands were first settled by the Polynesians, then "discovered" by Captain Cook, the English explorer. After Captain Cook visited in 1778, the call of the islands brought many and diverse groups— missionaries from the Boston area, sea-going men on whaling ships, English traders from India, and merchants from Spain and other parts. Each left its mark on the foods of the islands.

## Cuisine From Many Lands

The Polynesians brought pigs and chickens, bananas and taro. They, too, brought the coconut which has since become an important part of island industry and cuisine. The tops of their taro plants were the source of a favorite Hawaiian vegetable known as "luau". The tuberous roots, after being cooked and pounded to a pulp became "poi" — that famous (or infamous, depending on the viewpoint) food which the visitor aptly describes as wallpaper paste, but which has helped to develop many a happy, chubby and healthy baby.

The Chinese came to Hawaii to work on the sugar plantations. To them we owe the introduction of a fascinating array of vegetables — bean sprouts, lotus root, snow peas, bamboo shoots, water chestnuts, and wonderful leafy vegetables such as won bok cabbage and white or green mustard cabbage. From them we also learned to cut meat into bite-size pieces, to slice vegetables thinly and artistically, which was necessary for their quick "stir-fry" method of cooking. The result was nutritious, crisp, crunchy foods which lent themselves well to the Chinese style of eating with clicking chopsticks — from bowls rather than plates.

The Portuguese came to Hawaii from Europe about 1879 and soon put a lasting mark on the foods of the islands. Meals were perked up with the heady spices from the Azores and Madeira. Their sausages and beans made fabulous soups. The outdoor oven which soon appeared in the yard of the Portuguese home produced baked goods which have stood the test of time and are still among our most popular foods today . . . Portuguese Sweet Bread . . . ummm!

The early travelers from India are perhaps to be thanked for the popularity of the Hawaiian curry dinner. Through the years the skillful cooks of Hawaii developed a curry of their own — a dish to be proud of and one vastly different from the true Indian curry. Freshly made coconut milk formed the creamy highly spiced sauce for the meat or shellfish of their choice. Rice cooked in the Oriental manner — every grain dry and separate — was the bland base that tempered every spicy hot bite. But the crowning glories were the condiments which were the pride of the island hostess as she deftly presented them in her favorite condiment tray. No self-respecting hostess was without a least one prize tray — perhaps of lovely china or gleaming lacquer acquired from early traders. Today the compartmented condiment dish is apt to be carved from the wood of Hawaii's own Monkeypod tree.

The Japanese who also came to Hawaii to work on the plantations, brought a new way of cooking — on charcoal braziers, known as hichirin or hibachis. They brought new foods and added new flavors, but most of all they brought a heritage of artistry based on a quiet simplicity which has endured through the years in their foods, the decoration of their homes, and in fact, in most facets of their lives.

Later from the Orient came the Koreans whose foods were dominated by chili peppers, garlic and onions. Hot and spicy as the Korean foods were, we find they too have won their place among the current favorites. The redolent odor of Kim Chee has probably permeated the refrigerators of every race in Hawaii. And Kun Koki, the Korean broiled meat — ah, there is a treat which finds itself at home in dining room or backyard barbecue. Chunks of meat marinated in a sauce of soy, sugar and sesame oil, then broiled to a crispy, crusty brown is a dish which well deserves its crown of toasted sesame seeds.

In 1907 the Filipinos came and they also added their bit — new vegetables, new spices and their old standby — bagoong sauce. Their foods with the generous use of pimiento, tomatoes and spices were reminiscent of early Spanish recipes.

It was, incidentally, a Spaniard who mentioned in his early writings that he had planted pineapple in Hawaii in 1813; this pineapple, however, was of doubtful quality and it was the introduction of the Smooth Cayenne variety some fifty years later which was the beginning of the vast pineapple industry in Hawaii today.

# Entertaining Is Informal

Much of our island entertaining is informal, but it may run the gamut from backyard barbecue to drawing room elegance. It may be, as a hostess recently explained "Chinese food served French style". However, the informality of most homes in Hawaii and the casualness of dress make comfort and ease the keynote of the Hawaiian party. Most hostesses cook in many languages. Over the mock orange hedge (equivalent to over the back fence) recipes are exchanged as they are in any neighborly community; but in Hawaii the recipes reflect the mingling of many cultures. Mrs. Smith cherishes her new sukiyaki recipe while Mrs. Yamamoto may be equally thrilled to learn the secrets of Mrs. Smith's flaky pie crust.

As food is the universal language, it is no wonder that the many races of Hawaii live side by side in harmony, each sharing their customs and cultures and each benefitting equally from this interchange of ideas.

An invitation to dinner usually indicates the mood of the evening. "Come over for chop suey" suggests informality which in turn suggests muumuus for the ladies and aloha shirts for the men. Shoes — optional!

The nine-course Chinese dinner signifies an important occasion with a menu of many fabulous dishes. For any lesser occasion, however, the island hostess may select two or three of these delicious concoctions with which to build a menu for a family meal or a simple informal party.

Fortunate is the guest who is invited to a Japanese dinner and lucky indeed is the homemaker of another race who has mastered the art of Japanese cooking. To be a successful hostess in the Oriental manner she must also master the sincere hospitality of the Japanese people, their talent in flower arranging and their innate ability of making a beautiful picture from the materials at hand. A tray of ingredients — chopped meat or chicken, sliced vegetables, green onions tops tied in knots, mushrooms, bamboo shoots and water chestnuts — all the delectable goodies which go into sukiyaki are arranged with infinite care for color and shape contrast so as to present a perfect picture. Soon these ingredients are steaming away over the hichirin and the heavenly fragrance of soy sauce and ginger gives promise of the treat which lies ahead. This cooking is done at the table, first the meat is lightly sautéed, then the vegetables are added in the order of their sturdiness. Lastly, the quick cooking green onions, mushrooms and bean sprouts are added. The discerning cook, with a sniff or a sip, may decide to add a bit more soy or sugar at this point. Cubes of tofu (soybean curd) or long rice, which really isn't rice at all, but a vermicelli-like product made of mung beans, may also be added. Now the sukiyaki is ready to serve in exquisite lacquer or china bowls — to be eaten with chopsticks, of course. Sukiyaki, accompanied by tea and a wafer-like cookie (senbei) may be the complete menu, but it is often embellished with other delicacies. Tempura is a favorite and is any food which is batter coated and deep fried to a crispy goodness. Try parsley tempura sometime for a nice surprise — or cauliflower, green beans, or asparagus. And shrimp tempura, simply a glorified shrimp fritter, but what a fritter!

Japanese salads? Namasu is traditional and is one which is easy for the novice.

The popularity of Japanese teriyaki spread rapidly. No wonder — no one could resist the permeating fragrance of meat-on-a-stick as it wafted from the saimin stands of the past. Meat-on-a-stick is simply bits of beef, marinated in teriyaki sauce, threaded onto short bamboo sticks to be broiled briefly over charcoal. In the olden days, along with the meat sticks one could order a generous bowl of saimin for an extra dime. The humble, but picturesque curb-side stands, were the Japanese version of the American hamburger or pizza "parlor". Teriyaki sauce, we have found, also has an affinity for other meats — pork and lamb, as well as poultry and fish.

Saimin too, has come of age. This delicious broth and noodle soup is now found on the supermarket shelves in the "instant" version.

Neither Korean nor Filipino recipes have gained the universal appeal as that of the Oriental dishes in Hawaii. Korean Kun Koki and Kim Chee have been mentioned — both five-star performers. Likewise, we must mention Filipino favorites — Pansit, a noodle dish of distinction and Bakalaw, the native codfish stew, both being dishes which are relished by many.

All of Hawaii pays tribute to the Portuguese who introduced the incomparable Pao Doce, those round loaves of golden crustiness which are lighter than light. For the greatest enjoyment, this sweet, egg-rich bread should be eaten fresh from the oven. The accepted method it to "tear off a chunk and slither it generously with butter". Perfection in Portuguese baked goods is not easy for the in-experienced, so it is well that commercial bakeries have learned to produce these treats with old world flavor and quality.

# Story Of The Luau

No resume of Hawaii cuisine would be complete without the story of the luau (more correctly called the ahaaina). This feast of the islands is the perfect expression of Hawaiian hospitality.

The menu of the luau has remained essentially the same with minor variations. The star attraction is the kalua pig which is prepared in an underground oven or imu. The method is traditional — the cavity of a carefully cleaned fat porker is filled with large hot porous rocks as the carcass rests upon a bed of banana leaves supported on a basket-like piece of wire mesh. More banana leaves and stalks are placed over the pig, then basket and all is lowered into the imu — the pit which is also well filled with hot rocks. Laulaus, bananas and sweet potatoes are placed around the pig and all is covered with ti leaves, wet gunny sacks and soil. Hours of steaming result in a meal deluxe with an unforgettable flavor. Poi — the Hawaiian staff of life, lomi salmon, chicken luau, limu or seaweed, squid, opihis, and pipikaula (Hawaiian jerky) help round out the menu. For dessert one can usually select from several — coconut cake, haupia, or assorted island fruits.

Luau food is delicious although it may take a "bit of getting used to" by some, but food alone does not a luau make! It is the genial atmosphere, the music, the flowers, the colorful clothing and the lovely hula dancers that add the spell of romance to this time-honored Hawaiian feast.

An Imu is readied for cooking of traditional Kalua Pig at Duke Kahanamoku's Restaurant, International Market Place, Waikiki.

# Old American Favorites Too

You may wonder about the good, old American favorites, steak, French fries and apple pie! Aren't they served in Hawaii? Never fear, they have held their place in the menus of the islands. The early missionaries brought their favorite recipes and taught the natives to use many of them. Merchants, seamen and plantation men arrived with their wives and soon what may still be called "haole" (Caucasian) foods were made part of Hawaii's varied food pattern.

The traveller in Hawaii may eat a different type of food every day of the week or, if he lacks imagination, he may eat exactly as he does at home since fast air freight makes it possible for our modern supermarkets to offer delicacies from all parts of the world.

All of Hawaii's homemakers appreciate the bounteous fruits provided by nature — exotic fruits are plentiful and are available to all — often in their own backyards. Rich in color, fragrances and flavor are the year-round papayas, pineapple, coconuts, lemons and limes. More seasonal are the incomparable mangoes and avocados, the guavas and the passion fruit. More than one hundred tropical or subtropical fruits flourish in the islands although some are limited in supply such as the lychee, pohas, carissa, carambola, the sweetsop and the soursop. All the island fruits have found their way into brightening the menus of Hawaii's varied homemakers — in jams, jellies, sherbets, ice creams and sauces.

Come dine with us in Hawaii, meet our friends and neighbors and learn of their delightful customs. Share with us our fun and foods so that you too can say "Lucky we come Hawaii". Until you reach that lucky day, we hope you'll enjoy the many foods of Hawaii in your own home with the help of the suggestions and recipes in this book.

Mahalo and aloha nui,
Honolulu, Hawaii, 1965
Erma Meeks Boyen

# Substitutions For Hawaiian Foods

Before using these substitutes, check with your grocer. Many Hawaiian foods are now available in cans, jars, frozen and even fresh, via air freight, such as papayas.

Chinese parsley . . . . . . . . . . . . . . . . . . . . . . . . . . . . . . . . . . . . . . . parsley
Chinese Peas or snow peas . . . . . . . . . . . . . . . . . . . . . . . . tender green beans

Dried Mushrooms . . . . . . . . . . . . . . . . . . . . . . . . . . fresh or canned mushrooms

Ginger root (fresh) . . . . . . . . . . . . . . . . . . . . . . powdered ginger ( ⅓ as much)

Hawaiian salt . . . . . . . . . . . . . . . . . . . . . . . . . . . . . ice cream or rock salt
Heong liu fun . . . . . . . . . . . . . . . . . . . . . . . . . . . . . . . . . . . . . . . allspice

Linguica (Portuguese sausage) . . . . . . . . . . . . . . . . . any peppery-garlic sausage
Luau . . . . . . . . . . . . . . . . . . . . . . . . . . . . . . . . . . . . . . . . . . . . spinach

Macadamia nuts . . . . . . . . . . . . . . . . . . . . . . . . . . . . cashews or almonds
Mango . . . . . . . . . . . . . . . . . . . . . . . . . . . . . . . . . peach, fresh or canned

Nam yue (red bean curd) . . . . . . . . . . . . . . . . . . . . . . . . . no substitute (omit)

Papaya . . . . . . . . . . . . . . . . . . . . . . . . . . . . . . . . . . fresh peach or pear
Peanut oil . . . . . . . . . . . . . . . . . . . . . . . . . . . . . . . . . . . . . . . salad oil
Poi . . . . . . . . . . . . . . . . . . . . . . . . . . . . mashed bananas (really no substitute)

Saki . . . . . . . . . . . . . . . . . . . . . . . . . . . . . . . . dry white wine or flat beer

Taro . . . . . . . . . . . . . . . . . . . . . . . potato or sweet potato (really no substitute)
Taro leaves . . . . . . . . . . . . . . . . . . . . . . . . . . . . . . . . . . . . . . . . spinach
Ti leaves . . . . . . . . . . . . . . . . . . . . . . . . . . . . . . . . . . corn husks or foil

# PUPUS
## Appetizers & Dips

*"Pupus"* or *Hawaiian appetizers, as served at the Tahitian Lanai Restaurant.*

### MAUI LINGUICA — (Cheese & Sausage Broil)

½ lb. cheddar cheese, grated
¼ lb. linguica, chopped fine (spiced Italian or Mexican chorizo sausage)
1 egg, slightly beaten
Toast rounds

Blend cheese, linguica and egg in mixing bowl. Pile mixture on bread rounds (that have been toasted on one side). Place under broiler until bubbly and hot, approximately 4 to 5 mins. Serve hot. Makes about 3 dozen 2½-inch pupus.

## CHEESE 'N PINEAPPLE PUPUS

1 fresh pineapple, cubed
1¼ cups Luau Mayonnaise
   (see recipe)

1 cup grated Cheddar
   cheese
½ cup shredded coconut

Serve pineapple chunks on picks, with bowls of other ingredients. Dip pineapple first in mayonnaise, then in cheese and coconut.

## CANTONESE PINEAPPLE CUBES

Cantonese custom is to always place pineapple cubes in chilled salt water for 10 to 15 minutes before serving. The salt, according to Cantonese cooks, enhances the fresh flavor of the pineapple. Serve in shell of pineapple with long picks.

## WON TON (Crab Puffs)

**Won Ton Paste:**
2 cups flour (sifted before
   measuring)

1 tsp. salt
2 eggs, slightly beaten
2 to 4 tbs. water

Sift flour and salt into mixing bowl. Add eggs to flour and enough water to bind mixture together. Turn out on a floured board, knead till smooth. Cover and let stand for 15 minutes. Roll out very thin on floured board, cut into 3-inch squares.

**Crab Filling:**

2 3-oz. pkgs. cream cheese
2 green onions, minced
2 6-oz. cans of crab meat,
   shredded

Peanut oil (or salad oil)
   for frying

Cream the cheese, add crab meat and onions, blend well. Place Won Ton square in palm of hand with one corner pointed toward you. Place teaspoon of filling in center of square. Moisten four corners with egg or water and fold corner nearest you over to opposite corner. Press firmly to seal; fold third corner across its opposite side about ¾-inch below top points. Moisten and seal. Fold fourth corner across in the same way, moisten and seal. Cover and store in refrigerator until ready to cook. When ready to serve, fry a few at a time in deep hot oil, 375°F. until puffs are a golden brown and crab filling is hot.

## CHUTNEY TUNA PUPUS

1 7-oz. can tuna, drained
¾ cup mango chutney,
   finely chopped
¼ cup green pepper,
   finely chopped
¼ cup onion, minced

2/3 cup mayonnaise
Pastry for three 9-inch pie
   shells
1 egg, slightly beaten

Flake tuna with a fork and combine with chutney, green pepper, onions, and mayonnaise. Roll pastry to ⅛-inch thickness and cut into 2½-inch squares. Place 1 tsp. of tuna mixture in the center of each pastry square. Fold opposite corners together to form a triangle, pinching the edges together and sealing with the beaten egg. Cut small vents in top of pastry, brush with egg. Bake at 500°F. for 8 to 10 minutes. These pupus may be made a week ahead, stored in the freezer and baked, unthawed, just before serving. Yield: 5 dozen.

## PINEAPPLE - SHRIMP TEMPURA

10 prawns, uncooked or
   frozen (or 2½ to 3
   dozen large shrimp)
1 12-ounce can pineapple
   chunks
1½ cups sifted flour
1 tsp. plain or seasoned
   salt

½ cup water
1 egg, beaten
1 tsp. powdered ginger (or
   1 tbs. fresh grated ginger
   root)
Peanut oil (or salad oil)
   for frying

Remove shell and tail and devein prawns, cut each into thirds. If shrimps are used, leave whole. Drain pineapple, saving syrup. Skewer a piece of prawn (or shrimp) and a pineapple cube on small cocktail picks. Roll skewers in ½ cup of the flour mixed with ½ tsp. of the salt. Beat remaining flour and salt with water, ½ cup pineapple syrup, egg and ginger to a smooth batter. Dip floured skewers into batter, drain slightly and drop into heated shallow oil. Fry until richly browned turning once. The oil should be 1½-inches to 2-inches deep in skillet and about 350°F. If cooked prawns or shrimp are used, increase temperature to 370°F., as appetizers cook more quickly. Drain on rack or absorbent paper and keep hot till served. Serve plain or with any sauce, hot catsup or your favorite seafood dip. Yield: about 2½ to 3 dozen pupus.

## PIPIKALUA (Hawaiian Beef Jerky)

3 lbs. beef steak (well
marbled with fat)
1½ cups soy sauce
3 tbs. Hawaiian Salt or
ice cream salt)
2 tsp. sugar

1 clove garlic, minced
(optional)
1 tsp. vinegar or lemon juice
¼ tsp. monosodium
glutamate
¼ tsp. pepper

Cut steak into ¼-inch slices, then into ½-inch strips. Pound lightly to break up any tough tissue. Blend remaining ingredients and pour over meat and marinate 1 hour. Tie a string to the end of each piece and hang in hot sun one full day. Meat is now ready to be broiled to an even brown over charcoal or in an oven broiler. Uncooked meat may be stored in refrigerator until needed.

## ORIENTAL EGG ROLLS

1 large egg, beaten
1 cup lukewarm water
1 cup plus 2 tbs. flour
¼ cup cornstarch

½ tsp. salt
¼ tsp. almond extract
½ tsp. sugar

Combine ingredients and beat smooth. Heat a lightly oiled 10-inch skillet over low heat, pour and spread about 2 tbs. of batter to make a 5-inch square tissue-thin pancake. Use pastry brush to spread batter. Fill in holes by brushing more batter in the opposite direction. Fry on one side only. Repeat until all of batter is used. Set aside pancakes and make the following:

1 cup chopped cooked
chicken or flaked tuna
½ cup chopped bean
sprouts
½ cup chopped water
chestnuts
½ cup chopped bamboo
shoots

¼ cup chopped green
onions
¼ cup chopped green
pepper
1 tsp. grated ginger root
(or ginger juice)
¼ cup ground almonds
2 tsp. soy sauce

Mix all ingredients well. Spread a thin layer down the center of each pancake. Fold side edges over filling — roll carefully in jelly roll fashion. Seal open edge with batter or egg. Allow to dry. Fry in deep fat at 360°F. until brown, about 10 mins. Slice in 1½-inch pieces, and serve hot. Yield: 10 egg rolls.

## TEMPURA FISH BITS

Use recipe for Shrimp Tempura and substitute bite-size pieces of boneless white fish for shrimp. Serve on picks with a variety of dips.

## TOASTED COCONUT CHIPS

Remove meat from fresh coconut and slice paper thin with knife or potato peeler. Spread on cookie sheet and sprinkle with salt. Bake at 300° F. until golden brown (about 20 mins.), stirring twice to insure even cooking. Cool and store in air-tight container. Serve as pupus and with beverages.

## RUMAKI

1 lb. fresh chicken livers
1 tsp. salt
1 tsp. grated fresh ginger or
 ¼ tsp. powdered ginger
1 tsp. soy sauce

1 cup drained water
 chestnuts
16 slices bacon
1 cup salad oil

Cut livers into small bite-size pieces and season with salt, ginger and soy sauce. Cut water chestnuts and bacon in halves. Wrap one piece liver and chestnut in bacon and secure with pick. Heat oil in skillet and fry until golden brown. (Rumaki may also be broiled or baked in hot oven). Serve hot with fruit chutney, chili sauce, Chinese Mustard or Hot Shoyu Sauce (see recipes).

## WATER CHESTNUT-PINEAPPLE ROLL-UPS

1 lb. lean bacon
2½ cups water chestnuts

5 cups pineapple chunks

Cut bacon slices into thirds. Slice water chestnuts and drain pineapple thoroughly. Wrap a slice of water chestnut and a piece of pineapple in bacon. Secure with a food pick. Broil about 4 inches below flame turning once or twice until excess fat is removed and bacon is lightly browned. Set aside until fat has dripped off on paper towel. Place roll-ups on rack in a shallow baking pan. Just before serving, reheat in a 350°F. oven about 5 minutes. If these appetizers are prepared and frozen, thaw before broiling. Yield: About 5 dozen.

## LIME-SHRIMP COCKTAIL

1½ lbs. fresh raw shrimp,
   shelled and deveined
1 cup fresh lime juice
   (or bottled)

1 tbs. soy sauce
½ tsp. fresh ground pepper
¼ cup chopped onions
1½ cups chopped celery

Cut shrimp into bite-size pieces, wash and dry on absorbent paper. Mix remaining ingredients together, except for celery, and pour over shrimp. Marinate in refrigerator overnight. Serve in cocktail glasses or sherbet cups which have been lined with chopped celery. The lime juice "cooks" the shrimp so there is no "raw" flavor.

## SASHIMI (Raw Fish Cocktail)

1 lb. fresh sea bass, boned
   (or other fresh white-
   meated fish)
Shredded lettuce and
   crushed ice

¾ cup soy sauce
1½ tsp. grated ginger root
   (¼ tsp. ground ginger),
   or Oriental radish or
   dry mustard

Remove all skin and dark meat from boneless fish. Cut diagonally across the fish into very thin slices. Chill. Combine soy sauce and ginger in small bowl (if using other ingredients, such as dry mustard, use amount to your taste). Arrange fish on shredded lettuce and crushed ice. Using picks, dip into sauce. Makes about 2 dozen tidbits. A little sour cream or mayonnaise may be added to sauce for a creamy, milder flavor.

## SWEET 'N SOUR DIP FOR SHELLFISH

¾ cup sugar
1 tsp. salt
1 tsp. dry mustard
⅓ cup wine vinegar
1 cup salad oil

¼ tsp grated onion
2 tbs. green pepper, finely
   minced
2 tbs. pimiento, finely
   minced

Combine dry ingredients. Add vinegar and blend thoroughly. Boil mixture for 1 min. Cool thoroughly and add oil slowly, beating mixture until thickened. Add onion, green pepper and pimiento. Garnish top with slices of pimiento and small slice of green pepper. Excellent for shrimp, crab, lobster, etc. Yield: 1⅓ cups.

## HONOLULU DIP

½ cup crushed pineapple
2 tbs. chopped mint

3 oz. cream cheese
2 tbs. mayonnaise

Blend ingredients well. Serve in small bowls with hot fried celery sticks and, or, crackers.

## KIM CHEE DIP (Oriental Relish dip)

1 8-oz. pkg. cream cheese

2/3 cup Kim Chee (see recipe)

Soften cream cheese at room temperature. Beat, blending in Kim Chee. If commercial Kim Chee is too coarse, chop before adding to cream cheese. Taste, add extra red pepper if desired. Makes about 1½ cups of dip. Serve with chips or crackers.

## LUAU FRUIT BITS

Cut fresh pineapple and papaya in bite-size pieces and serve on picks with Luau Mayonnaise dip (see recipe).

## SOY DAIKON BITS

1½ lbs. daikon (Japanese
  white radish)
1 cup soy sauce
½ tsp. monosodium
  glutamate

¼ tsp. grated fresh ginger
  root (or dash of dry
  ground ginger)

Wash and peel daikon and cut into small bite-size pieces. Blend remaining ingredients and pour over daikon. Refrigerate overnight (will keep several days) and serve chilled.

## CHINESE MUSTARD

Mix till smooth, ⅓ cup dry mustard, 1 tbs. salad oil, 1 tsp. sugar, ½ tsp. salt and 2 tbs. water (flat beer or wine, Saki is best). Serve in small dipping bowl.

## CHUTNEY & CURRY MAYONNAISE

To 1 cup mayonnaise, blend 1 tbs. minced fruit chutney and 1 tsp. curry powder, for a spicy dip for seafoods and chicken salad.

## COLD SHOYU (SOY) SAUCE

½ cup soy sauce
3 tbs. brown sugar

2 tbs. wine vinegar

Blend ingredients well. Serve in small bowls with hot fried foods, or cold meat and fish pupus.

## HOT SHOYU (SOY) SAUCE

1 cup soy sauce
2/3 cup water
½ cup brown sugar

1 tsp. grated onion
2 tsp. corn starch

Blend all ingredients and heat to a light boil. Serve as dip for Shrimp Tempura, pupus or as a sauce for fish or chicken.

## GOLDEN SHOYU DIP

1 cup mayonnaise
¼ cup soy sauce

½ tsp. grated onion
(optional)
½ tsp. lemon juice

Blend ingredients till smooth. Chill and re-stir before serving as dip for all fish "pupus" or with grilled or fried fish.

## LUAU MAYONNAISE

Thin 1 cup mayonnaise with 2 tbs. pineapple juice or syrup and 1 tbs. maraschino cherry syrup. Blend to a smooth pink color.

# SOUPS & SAUCES

*Watercress Soup is a deliciously different Hawaiian meal favorite.*

## POLYNESIAN WATERCRESS SOUP

3 tbs. butter or margarine
3 tbs. flour
¾ tsp. salt
¼ to ½ tsp. curry powder
3 cups milk
1½ cups shredded carrot

½ cup boiling water
¾ cup chopped watercress
Papaya, cut in cubes
Macadamia nuts
Shredded coconut

Melt butter in sauce pan; blend in flour, salt and curry powder. Gradually stir in milk and cook, stirring constantly, till smooth and thickened. Set aside. Put carrots in boiling water in a small sauce pan; cook covered, about 3 minutes or until just tender. Chop washed watercress using green part of stems as well as the leaves. Add to carrots and cook about ½ minute longer. Stir carrots and watercress into hot milk mixture; bring just to simmering point. Serve immediately with suggested condiments.

## WATERCRESS SOUP

3 cups milk
2 cups watercress, chopped
1 small onion, diced
2 cups potatoes, diced
  and cooked

1 tsp. Worcestershire sauce
½ tsp. salt
¼ tsp. monosodium
  glutamate
Dash of pepper

Pour 2 cups of the milk into blender, add watercress, onion, and potatoes and blend thoroughly. Pour into a saucepan, add remaining milk, cook over low heat for about 25 minutes, stirring occasionally. Add remaining ingredients and serve immediately.

## CREAM OF AVOCADO SOUP

1 cup sieved avocado
1½ cups chicken broth
½ cup heavy cream

1 tbs. sherry wine
½ small avocado, diced
Whipped cream

Pour broth in sauce pan and add avocado pulp. Slowly bring to the boiling point (but do not boil). Add cream and again slowly heat to boiling, stirring so as not to burn. Add sherry and remove from heat. Place a tbs. of diced avocado in each bouillon cup, fill cup with soup. Top with salted whipped cream and serve immediately.

## MOCK BIRD'S NEST SOUP

1 bundle long rice (from
  Chinese market)
4 dried mushrooms (fresh
  or canned may be used)
6 cups chicken broth
⅛ tsp. monosodium
  glutamate
1½ tsp. salt

1 cup ground pork
½ cup ground ham
½ cup water chestnuts,
  chopped
2 egg whites, slightly
  beaten
Chopped Chinese parsley
  (coriander or parsley)

Cut long rice with scissors in ¼-inch lengths and soak in hot water for 30 minutes. Soak dried mushrooms in warm water until soft; wash thoroughly and remove stems, finely chop caps. To the broth add mushrooms, seasonings, meat and water chestnuts, simmer for 30 minutes. Add drained long rice and simmer 5 mins. more. Remove from heat and stir in egg whites. Serve hot with chopped parsley sprinkled on top of each bowl. When using fresh mushrooms, add during last 5 minutes of cooking. A quick and easy way to cut the long rice is to place 4-inch lengths in electric blender, switch on and off until chopped fine.

## COCO-LOBSTER SOUP

2 cups cooked lobster, cut to bite-size
3½ cups coconut milk (see recipe)
1 tsp. soy sauce
Dash of Tabasco sauce
Chopped parsley
2 tbs. sherry wine (optional)

Combine lobster meat with all of the remaining ingredients. Cook over a low heat for about 15 minutes, but do not boil. Add sherry last 3 mins. of cooking. Serve immediately, garnish each bowl with sprinkling of parsley. This delightful soup may be served chilled.

## NATIVE CODFISH STEW

1 lb. salted codfish
1 clove garlic
2 tbs. shortening (or margarine)
2 medium onions, sliced
1½ cups potatoes, diced
2 cups canned tomatoes
2 tsp. chopped parsley
½ cup water
1 pkg. frozen peas

Wash and soak codfish in water overnight. Drain; separate into small pieces removing bones and skin. Brown garlic in shortening and remove from pan. Add codfish and cook for a few minutes. Add remaining ingredients, cover and simmer for 30 minutes.

## PORTUGUESE KAU KAU (Pink Bean Soup)

2 cups red or pink beans
2 qts. boiling water
1 medium onion, sliced
1 linguica (Italian pepper sausage or chorizo sausage)
1 carrot, diced
1 turnip, diced
2 potatoes, diced
1 small cabbage, chopped
1 can tomato sauce
1 to 2 qts. water
3 tbs. salt

Wash beans, cover with boiling water and soak an hour or more. Add onion and skinned sausage. Cook until beans are tender (about 1 hour). Add remaining ingredients and simmer another hour and a half.

VARIATIONS: 1 lb. of cubed beef brisket may be cooked with the beans. When preparing soup without meat or sausage, include a clove of garlic, 1 tbs. salad oil, ⅛ tsp. pepper and a dash of cayenne. Sweet potatoes may be substituted for white potatoes.

## TOMATO CURRY SOUP

1 8-oz. can creamed corn
1 can tomato soup
1 cup milk
½ to 1 tsp. curry powder

Dash of pepper
¼ tsp. salt
Parsley, finely chopped

Put creamed corn in blender, cover and blend at high speed for one minute. Add remaining ingredients, and blend for another minute. Pour into sauce pan and heat on low flame, stirring occasionally. When hot, pour into serving bowls and sprinkle with parsley.

## COCONUT MILK (for recipes)

Pour 1½ cups boiling milk over 1½ cups fresh or dry grated coconut. Let stand 20 mins. and strain liquids, pressing with a spoon to separate as much milk as possible. Do not confuse with liquid found in fresh mature coconuts; use in all recipes calling for "coconut milk."

## COCONUT CREAM

1 cup coconut milk (see recipe)

Allow the coconut milk to set for a few hours in the refrigerator or cool place. A thick, creamy substance will rise to the top and may be skimmed off. This coconut cream may be served as a sauce for pudding, or it may be whipped when thoroughly chilled.

## MACADAMIA NUT SAUCE

¼ cup butter
¼ cup Hawaiian
   macadamia nuts, sliced

1 tbs. parsley, chopped
1 tsp. fresh lemon juice
Sprinkle of nutmeg

Melt butter slowly in skillet, until butter, oil and curd is separated. Spoon off the oil, which is drawn butter. Sauté nuts in the drawn butter until just golden brown. Stir in remaining ingredients and serve over sautéed fish fillets.

## ONO ONO VEGETABLE SAUCE

3 tbs. butter (or margarine)
3 tbs. flour
dash pepper

¾ cup milk or buttermilk
3 tbs. soy sauce
½ cup mayonnaise

Melt butter in top of double boiler. Blend in flour and pepper. Add milk and soy sauce and cook over boiling water until mixture is smooth and thickened, stirring constantly. Blend in mayonnaise with gentle stirring, and continue cooking briefly until hot. Pour over lightly cooked green beans, asparagus, cabbage or broccoli. Garnish with paprika or chopped Hawaiian macadamia nuts. (Ono Ono means delicious in Hawaiian — and this unique sauce is!)

## HAWAIIAN CURRY SAUCE

¼ cup salad oil
1 onion, minced
2 apples, pared and diced
5 tbs. flour
1 tsp. curry powder*

2 cups Coconut Milk (see recipe) or milk
1 tsp. salt
1 tsp. ground ginger
3 tbs. soy sauce

Heat oil and add onions and apples. Cover and cook 10 mins., stirring occasionally. Add flour and stir until smooth. Add coconut milk or milk along with salt, ginger, curry powder and soy sauce, stirring constantly till mixture thickens and boils. Reduce heat to very low, cover and cook 20 mins. Sauce is now ready to be mixed with 2 cups cooked seafood, chicken or meat and served on steamed rice, or as called for in recipes. *Curry powder comes in a variety of strengths. Start with 1 tsp., more can be added to taste.

## TROPICAL FRUIT SYRUP (for pancakes and desserts)

1 cup pineapple or orange juice or (tropical fruit nectars)

1½ cups sugar
Juice of 1 lemon, or lime

In sauce pan, combine all ingredients and bring to slow boil. Simmer to consistency of syrup. May be used hot. Store in covered jar in refrigerator, will keep for weeks.

## TERIYAKI MARINADE FOR MEATS

½ cup shoyu (soy sauce)
¼ cup Bourbon (or sherry wine)
2 tbs. brown sugar

Dash of dry mustard
1 clove garlic, crushed
1 tbs. fresh ground ginger (or ½ tsp. ginger powder)

Mix all ingredients together until sugar is dissolved. Pour into a shallow dish large enough to hold either meat or chicken. Marinate for at least 1 hour (longer if possible), turning pieces at least two or three times. Drain before broiling. Use the marinade to baste during cooking. Suggested meats for Teriyaki are: Chicken, rib-eye or other tender cuts of beef. For Teriyaki-Hawaiian style, each guest spears marinated beef cubes on skewer alternating with water chestnut wrapped in bacon and broils over table hibachi. Heat remaining marinade until just warm and serve for a dipping sauce.

*USE HAWAIIAN JAMS AND JELLIES . . .*

The fragrance and color of the fruits of the Islands are captured for your table in Hawaiian Jams and Jellies. Jewel-toned guava jelly and jam, golden papaya-pineapple jam, unique poha preserves, zesty and distinctive mango chutney and the smooth deliciousness of coconut syrup are all nostalgic reminders of Hawaii.

- Use your imagination to create "Island ways" for many menus.
- Jelly glazes for meats, give a most unusual flavor and appetite appeal.
- Fill butter biscuits with named types of Hawaiian jams and jellies before baking.
- Have a "Hawaiian Sundae" dessert party — different and delectable.

Make breakfast special — English muffins with Hawaiian jellies — coconut syrup over hotcakes and waffles — a dab of guava jelly in that broiled grapefruit half — mango chutney to enhance a beautiful omelette.

# SALADS & DRESSINGS

*Add zip to fresh Hawaiian fruit salads with Papaya Seed Dressing.*

## HAWAIIAN FRUIT BOAT

1 large fresh pineapple
1 papaya, cut in 1-inch
   cubes
2 bananas, sliced

½ cup freshly grated
   coconut (or ½ cup
   flaked coconut)
2 ozs. Kirsch (optional),
   can substitute light rum

Lay pineapple on side. Cutting lengthwise, cut one-third of the
pineapple off, beginning at the bottom of the fruit and cutting
through top as well. Remove fruit from the pineapple shell by
first removing the core down the center. The balance of the
fruit may be easily removed by using a grapefruit knife and
cutting around the fruit and about ¾ inches from the skin.
Cube pineapple, add papaya, Kirsch and chill. Just before
serving, add sliced bananas and mix gently. Place in chilled
pineapple "boat" and top with grated coconut. A few vanda
orchids may be added for color.

## CURRIED CHICKEN - TOMATO SALAD

3 lbs. chicken, cooked
½ cup diced celery
1 cup pineapple chunks
2 tsp. grated onion
½ cup seedless grapes,
  halved
⅓ cup chopped Hawaiian
  macadamia nuts

1 to 2 tsp. curry powder
1 cup mayonnaise
1 tsp. salt
Dash of pepper
6 firm tomatoes
Lettuce leaves

Remove chicken meat from bones and dice. Add celery, pineapple chunks, onion, grapes and nuts. Combine curry, mayonnaise and seasonings and stir into chicken mixture. Chill. Cut tomatoes in sixths, almost but not quite through to form petal shape. Place on lettuce leaves and fill with chilled salad mixture.

## CHINESE CHICKEN SALAD MAGNIFICENT

¼ cup soy sauce
1 tsp. fresh ginger root,
  grated
½ tsp. garlic salt
¼ tsp. sugar
4 chicken breasts, boned
  pieces
1 head lettuce,
  torn in pieces
¾ cup sliced celery
¼ cup green onions,
  slivered and cut in
  1-inch pieces

½ cup chopped parsley
½ cup chopped Hawaiian
  macadamia nuts or
  cashews
1 tbs. toasted sesame
  seeds
1 cup crushed potato chips
¼ cup salad oil
¼ tsp. celery salt
¼ tsp. pepper
¼ tsp. salt
Dash coarse pepper

Combine soy sauce, ginger, garlic salt and sugar. Marinate chicken in mixture at least 1 hour, turning frequently. Deep fat fry about 3 minutes, drain and cool on absorbent paper. Cut chicken into slivers. Toss vegetables in salad bowl and top with nuts, sesame seeds, potato chips and chicken slivers. Combine salad oil, celery salt, salt and pepper and sprinkle over salad just before serving.

## CUCUMBER SALAD (Kiyuri Namasu)

3 cups very thinly sliced
  cucumbers
½ tsp. salt
1 tsp. finely chopped
  ginger root (¼ tsp.
  ground ginger)

½ cup white wine vinegar
2 tbs. sugar
¼ tsp. monosodium
  glutamate

Partly peel cucumbers leaving strips of green, and slice very thin. Add salt to cucumbers and let stand for 15 minutes. Combine remaining ingredients. Press excess liquid from cucumbers and add to sauce. Chill and serve as a relish or salad. Sometimes small pieces of thinly sliced mushrooms, carrots, or abalone are added to this relish.

## PINEAPPLE CHICKEN SALAD

2 cups cubed cooked
  chicken
2 cups cubed fresh
  pineapple
½ cup mayonnaise

1 cup diced celery
½ cup chopped Hawaiian
  macadamia nuts,
  almonds or mixed nuts

Chill all ingredients and combine, tossing lightly. Garnish with additional nuts and watercress.

## LYCHEE SALAD MOLD

1½ cups grapefruit sections
  (or mandarin oranges)
1 10-oz. can lychees
1 tsp. unflavored gelatin

1 pkg. orange gelatin
1 pkg. lemon gelatin
Cold water

Thoroughly drain canned fruits, saving the liquids. Add enough cold water to the liquids to make 3½ cups. Soften unflavored gelatin in ¼ cup of the liquid. Pour remaining liquid into saucepan and heat to boiling point. Combine the softened gelatin and the 2 flavored gelatins in a bowl and mix well, add boiling liquid, stirring to dissolve gelatins. Cool thoroughly, add grapefruit or oranges and the halved, seeded lychees. Pour into a well oiled 1 qt. ring mold and chill until completely set. If desired, fill center of the unmolded ring with Curried Chicken Salad (see recipe) substituting diced tart apples for the pineapple and slivered toasted almonds for the macadamia nuts.

## HAWAIIAN PINEAPPLE - AVOCADO SALAD

2 cups pineapple slices,
   drained
Paprika
3 large avocados, sliced
   lengthwise

¼ cup water
Juice of 1 lemon
Salad greens

Cut each pineapple slice into 4 pieces. Dip the rim of each piece into paprika. Dip sliced avocado pieces into solution of water and lemon juice. Place salad greens in large salad bowl (or individual bowls) and arrange the avocado and pineapple slices in a single layer alternating sections or pinwheel fashion. Serve with Chutney Dressing (see recipe).


## TROPIC MANGO SALAD

1½ cups sliced fresh
   mango
1 cup sliced banana
1 cup sliced orange
6 lettuce leaves

Juice of 1 lime
2 tbs. honey
¼ cup salad oil
⅛ tsp. salt
6 maraschino cherries

Place fruit in mixing bowl and chill. Blend lime juice with honey, then add salad oil and salt. Pour over fruit and mix gently so as not to break the fruit. Place lettuce leaves in individual salad bowls and fill with fruit. Pour extra dressing over top, garnish with cherry and serve chilled.


## SEAFOAM SALAD

1 pkg. lemon gelatin
1 cup hot water
3 tbs. lemon juice
1 tsp. salt
½ cup mayonnaise

1 cup sieved avocado pulp
½ cup heavy cream,
   whipped
Lettuce leaves

Dissolve gelatin in hot water. Cool and add lemon juice and salt. Chill until mixture begins to thicken. Fold in mayonnaise, avocado, and whipped cream which have been blended together. Pour into an oiled ring mold and chill until firm. Unmold on lettuce leaves.
Seafoam salad may be varied through the choice of garnish. Use mandarin oranges and grapefruit sections for a light salad and marinated shrimp or lobster for a heartier salad.

## PINEAPPLE FRUIT BOATS

Cut a whole fresh pineapple from bottom to top, including the leaves. Remove fruit from center, leaving a ¾-inch shell. Dice pineapple meat and blend with diced fresh papaya, banana and orange. Refill shells, chill and top with Luau Mayonnaise or Papaya Seed Dressing (see recipes).

## SANDWICH ISLANDS LOBSTER SALAD

2 cups cooked shell
   macaroni
1 cup cooked lobster, diced

1 cup cooked carrots, diced
1 cup celery, diced
2/3 cup mayonnaise

Combine ingredients and chill. Serve garnished with minced parsley and paprika.

## TOMATO, PINEAPPLE & PEANUT SALAD

6 medium tomatoes
½ tsp. salt
1 cup crushed pineapple
⅓ cup chopped peanuts

⅓ cup diced celery
2 tbs. French dressing
6 lettuce leaves

Cut a slice from the top of each tomato and remove some of the pulp. Drain the tomatoes and sprinkle with salt. Chill thoroughly. Dice tomato pulp and combine with drained pineapple, peanuts, celery and French dressing. Place in cavity of the tomatoes and chill. Arrange on lettuce leaves.

## CHUTNEY DRESSING

1 cup salad oil
⅓ cup wine vinegar
1 clove garlic, crushed
1 tsp. salt

¼ tsp. monosodium
   glutamate
1 cup chutney, finely
   chopped

Mix all ingredients in a jar, shake well and store in refrigerator until ready to use. Shake well before serving with mixed green salad, fruit, or may be used as a dip.

## HAWAIIAN FRENCH DRESSING

¼ cup white wine vinegar
¾ cup salad oil
1 tsp. salt
¼ tsp. monosodium
   glutamate
½ tsp. dry mustard

1 tsp. sugar
¼ tsp. ground pepper
¼ cup pineapple juice or
   crushed fresh pineapple
¼ cup minced fresh mint

Blend vinegar with dry ingredients before mixing in oil, pineapple and mint. Shake in a closed jar and chill before using. Excellent on both green and fruit salads.

## PAPAYA SEED DRESSING

1 cup sugar
1 tbs. salt
1 tsp. dry mustard
1 cup white wine or
   tarragon vinegar

1 cups salad oil
1 small onion, chopped
3 tbs. fresh papaya seeds

Place all dry ingredients and vinegar in blender. Turn on blender and gradually add salad oil and onion. When thoroughly blended, add papaya seeds. Blend only until seeds are the size of coarse ground pepper. The piquant flavor of this dressing is excellent for either fruit or tossed green salads. Makes 3 cups.

## SESAME SEED DRESSING

¾ cup sugar (or less)
¼ tsp. dry mustard
½ tsp. paprika
½ tsp. salt
¼ tsp. Tabasco sauce
¼ tsp. Worcestershire
   sauce

¾ tbs. minced onion
1 cup salad oil
½ cup wine vinegar
¼ cup toasted sesame
   seeds

Combine all ingredients in blender container and blend thoroughly. May be stored in refrigerator. If dressing separates, blend briefly before serving on mixed greens or fruit salads.

# SEAFOODS

*A Pacific favorite, Shrimp Tempura is made easily from few ingredients.*

## SHRIMP TEMPURA

1½ lbs. large shrimp,
   fresh or frozen
½ cup corn starch
½ cup flour
1 tsp. salt

¼ tsp. monosodium
   glutamate
1 egg
½ cup water
1½ cups salad oil

Shell and clean shrimp leaving tails on. Split shrimp through back, cutting almost through; open to butterfly shape. Sift dry ingredients together. Beat egg with water. Blend both together for batter. Heat oil to 375°F., dip shrimp through batter holding tail and drop gently into oil. When shrimps rise to surface, turn and continue cooking until golden brown. Drain on paper towel and serve immediately with Hot Shoyu Sauce (see recipe) or Chinese Mustard.

## MAUI PICKLED SHRIMP

1½ lbs. cleaned cooked
   shrimp
½ cup minced parsley
1 onion, minced
1 clove garlic, minced

¼ cup salad oil
⅓ cup white wine vinegar
1 tsp. salt
dash pepper

Place shrimp, parsley and onion in a bowl. Blend together other ingredients and pour over shrimp. Chill at least an hour before serving (overnight is best) stirring once or twice. To serve, line a tray with ti leaves or what have you, and set a small bowl of chinese mustard (see recipe) in center. Heap drained shrimp around bowl and garnish with flowers. Use picks to dunk through sauce. (Maui Pickled Shrimp may also be served hot. Just skewer shrimp and barbecue only till hot. Use same dip).

## PINEAPPLE SHRIMP

1 cup fresh pineapple
   juice
1 cup fresh pineapple
   chunks
½ cup vinegar
½ cup tomato paste
1 cup sugar
1 cup water
1 tsp. salt
½ fresh green pepper (cut
   in large pieces)

½ small onion, cut in
   large pieces
1 cup flour
½ tsp. sugar
½ tsp. salt
1 egg
1 cup ice water
2 cups peanut oil (or salad
   oil)
2 lbs. fresh shrimp
2 tbs. cornstarch
½ cup water

Combine the first 9 ingredients in a saucepan, bring to boil and remove from heat. In a bowl, mix flour, ½ tsp. sugar, salt, egg, ice water to make a smooth batter. Peel shell from shrimp, leaving last section and tail intact. Slit in half lengthwise without removing either end; remove black line. Dry shrimp thoroughly, dip in batter and deepfat fry in peanut oil. Drain on absorbent paper. Thicken sauce with cornstarch mixed with ½ cup water, bring to boil. Remove from heat and pour over shrimp. Serves 6.

## OYSTER & NUT FRITTERS

4 eggs, beaten until
  frothy
¼ tsp. pepper
½ tsp. seasoned salt
¼ tsp. monosodium
  glutamate
1 green onion, chopped
  fine

¼ cup flour
¼ cup ground Hawaiian
  macadamia nuts
  (almonds or peanuts)
1½ cups oysters, cut in
  small pieces
Peanut oil (or salad oil)
  for frying

Mix all ingredients together, except oil, and blend well. Heat oil in skillet for deep frying, about 370°F. Drop oyster mixture in by tablespoonful, carefully so as not to splatter. Fry until golden brown on all sides. Drain on absorbent paper and serve immediately with bowl of Chinese Mustard, Hot Shoyu Sauce (see recipes) or chili sauce. Garnish with lemon or lime wedges.

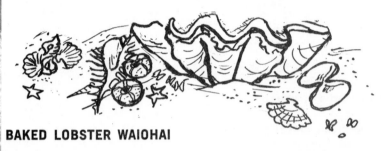

## BAKED LOBSTER WAIOHAI

6 lobster tails
2 cups sake (or dry white
  wine)
1 tsp. salt
Dash cayenne
½ cup butter
½ cup diced water
  chestnuts
½ cup diced bamboo
  shoots

½ cup diced celery
½ cup diced romaine
  lettuce
2 tbs. chili sauce
2 tbs. chopped parsley
3 tbs. French dressing
1 tsp. Worchestershire
  sauce
1½ cups mayonnaise
½ cup catsup

Remove lobster from shell and dice. Season with salt, marinate in sake for 1 hour. Drain. Heat butter in skillet, sauté lobster about 12 minutes. Cool. Mix following ingredients together in bowl: water chestnuts, bamboo shoots, celery, lettuce, chili sauce, parsley, French dressing and Worcestershire sauce. Stir in cooled lobster, fill shells with this mixture. Mix the mayonnaise and catsup together, pour over top. Bake in hot oven (400°F.) for 10 minutes or until brown. Garnish with wedge of lime (or lemon).

## SEAFOOD CURRY IN PAPAYA

Heat 1½ lbs. cooked and cubed crab, lobster or shrimp with Hawaiian Curry Sauce (see recipe). Cut fresh papaya in half lengthwise (a half per serving) and scoop out seeds. Peel and and fill with seafood mixture and broil or bake in hot oven till lightly browned on top. Serve topped with chopped nuts, chutney and minced parsley.

## PAPAYA 'N CRAB MEAT SUPREME

1 6½-oz. can crab meat,
  flaked
2/3 cup celery, thinly
  sliced

½ cup toasted slivered
  almonds
2 fresh papayas, chilled
Fresh lime or lemon juice

Mix crab meat and celery and chill. Cut papayas in half and scoop out seeds with teaspoon. Peel papaya halves and place on individual shell plates or salad plates. Sprinkle crab meat and celery with juice of a fresh lime, add slivered almonds and pile in papaya halves. Garnish with sprig of parsley and serve with additional wedge of lime.

## FISH & YAM FRITTERS

1½ lbs. fish fillets
  (halibut, whitefish or
  sole)
1 small onion, chopped
2 tsp. seasoned salt
½ tsp. white pepper
½ tsp. monosodium
  glutamate

1 cup flat beer or water
2½ cups yams or sweet
  potatoes, cooked and
  mashed
⅓ cup light cream
1 egg, beaten
½ cup flour
Oil for deep frying

Simmer the fish, onion, 1 tsp. seasoned salt, pepper and monosodium glutamate in beer until fish is "flake" done (about 20 minutes). Drain, and when fish and onion mixture is cool, flake with fork. Beat the yams, cream, and 1 tsp. seasoned salt until fluffy. Blend with fish mixture. Roll into 2-inch balls and dust with flour. Heat oil in skillet and fry at 375°F. until fritters are browned. Drain on absorbent paper and serve immediately. Garnish with watercress or parsley, and wedge of lemon.

## FISH BAKED IN TI LEAVES

3 to 5 lb. fish (whole and
 cleaned)
1 tsp. salt
1 tbs. onion, minced
1 tsp. parsley, minced
1 tbs. bacon drippings
½ tsp. salt

Dash of pepper
1 cup small bread cubes
¼ cup milk or broth
3 slices bacon
Ti leaves (Corn husks or
 foil)

Rub the inside of fish with salt. Let stand 5 minutes. Blend together onion, parsley, bacon drippings, seasonings, bread cubes and liquid. Lightly stuff fish with mixture. Sew fish together with string or secure with skewers. Arrange slices of bacon over the top. Wrap in ti leaves and place in oiled baking pan. Bake at 325°F., for 20 minutes per pound.

## LAU LAUS

1 lb. taro or fresh spinach
 leaves
1½ lbs. shredded pork
 (beef, lamb or chicken
 may be used)
1½ lbs. boneless white
 fish, shredded
1 tsp. monosodium
 glutamate

2 tbs. Hawaiian salt or ice
 cream salt
1 cube butter (or
 margarine) melted
12 ti leaves (or banana
 leaves, corn husks or
 foil)

Wash and trim taro or spinach leaves. Place pork pieces in bowl and work in salt and monosodium glutamate. Pour butter (or margarine) over fish pieces. Place about 5 taro or spinach leaves in the palm of one hand and top with a medium handful of pork and fish. Wrap the leaves up over the sides of the mixture and join at top to form a package. Now place this bundle upside down at one end of a de-veined ti leaf (banana leaf or several corn husks or foil) and roll into a tight package. Additional leaves may be required to cover all sides. Tie with string. Steam packages 4-6 hours (Hawaiian style) or pressure cook with ½ cup water 20 min. Serve Lau Laus whole, garnished with a flower, allowing each guest to unwrap his own.

## FISH STEAKS IN BEER

1½ lbs. boneless fish
    steaks
2 cans beer
1 onion
1 lemon
2 bay leaves

2 tbs. butter
2 tbs. flour
½ tsp. paprika
½ tsp. seasoned salt
⅛ tsp. pepper

Lay fish steaks in a heavy sauce pan with a cover. Pour over beer, add onion, lemon cut in half, bay leaves, paprika and seasoned salt. Bring to a boil and turn heat to low, cover and simmer 5 minutes. Remove cover and simmer 5 minutes longer. Lift fish steaks out of broth and discard onion, lemon and bay leaves. Blend the butter and flour into a smooth paste and add to broth, stirring constantly until sauce boils and thickens. Add pepper and fish steaks to sauce and simmer just long enough to reheat fish. Serve immediately with rice or noodles.

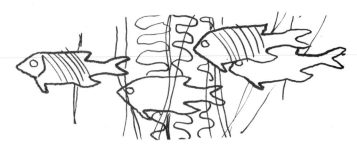

## AHI (Fish for 12)

2¼ lbs. Ahi (fish, use
    fillet of halibut or white
    sea bass)
25 limes or 1½ cups
    bottled lime juice
2 qts. Coconut Milk (see
    recipe)

Peelings of 1 cucumber,
    finely chopped
1 small carrot, grated
½ cup salt
½ cup chopped green
    onion
Romaine lettuce leaves

Dice Ahi into ¼-inch cubes, add salt. Add water to cover fish and let stand while squeezing limes. Then add juice to fish and water and let marinate, at least overnight in refrigerator. The lime juice "cooks" the fish, taking away the raw flavor. Combine coconut milk and remaining ingredients, chill. A half hour before serving, drain fish and combine with coconut milk mixture and place in refrigerator. Serve chilled in individual serving bowls lined with romaine. Garnish with finely chopped hard cooked eggs.

## BAKED SEAFOOD WITH VEGETABLES

1 lb. medium size shrimps
1 6-oz. can crab meat
1 cup mayonnaise
2 carrots
3 stalks celery, sliced
2 green onions, cut 1-inch
   in lengths

1 tsp. salt
1 tsp. Worchestershire
   sauce
1 cup grated cheese or
   bread crumbs

Clean shrimp and cut them in half, lengthwise. Take bones out of crab meat. Cut carrots in 1-inch strips, about ½-inch wide and ¼-inch thick. Mix all ingredients together and put in baking dish. Sprinkle with cheese or bread crumbs and dot with butter. Bake in oven at 350°F. for 1 hour.

## GRILLED MAHI MAHI

1½ lbs. mahi mahi steaks
   (halibut or sole)
¼ lb. butter (or margarine)
1 tsp. salad oil

¼ tsp. garlic salt
1 tsp. soy sauce
½ tsp. lemon juice

Melt butter (or margarine) and pour over fish along with other ingredients. Marinate 30 mins. Grill over charcoal until fish is "flake" done. Serve with lemon slice and parsley sprig (or watercress).

## BUTTER WINE BAKED FISH

1½ lbs. boneless fish
   fillets or steaks
2 cups dry sherry wine or
   white table wine
½ cup flour

2 tbs. butter or margarine
1 onion sliced
½ tsp. salt
⅛ tsp. pepper
⅛ tsp. paprika

A half hour before cooking, place fish in a dish and pour over wine. If not completely covered, turn the fish after 15 minutes. Remove fish and save liquid for sauce. Dust fish with flour. In a heavy skillet with a cover, heat oil or butter and brown fish lightly on both sides. Add onion, wine liquid, salt, pepper and paprika. Cover and simmer 5 minutes. Remove from heat but do not uncover for 5 minutes longer (to steam fish). Serve with rice or noodles, garnished with parsley or watercress and lemon wedges, spooning remaining juice over fish as sauce.

# LOMI SALMON

1 lb. salted salmon*
5 tomatoes, peeled
   and diced

8 whole green onions,
   chopped
1 med. onion, chopped
½ cup crushed ice

Soak salmon in cold water 3 hrs. Remove skin and bones and shred finely. Combine all ingredients but ice and chill. Add ice just before serving in small bowls or hollowed tomatoes.
*Fresh, frozen or canned salmon may be used; disregard soaking.

# COCONUT TUNA

3 tbs. shortening
6 tbs. flour
3 cups milk
2 7-oz. cans tuna, flaked
1 tbs. pimiento, cut in
   strips

½ tsp. salt
Dash of pepper
1 cup diced canned
   pineapple
3 coconuts

Make a white sauce with the shortening, flour, and milk. Add remaining ingredients (except coconut) and mix well. Sandpaper off rough fiber of coconut shells and saw in half crosswise. Fill the halves with tuna mixture, place in shallow baking pan and bake at 350°F. for 1 hour. Garnish with sprig of parsley or watercress.

# HILO FILLET OF SOLE

1½ lbs. sole fillets
   (boneless)
¼ tsp. salt
2 tsp. grated onion
1½ tsp. water
¾ cup mayonnaise

1 tsp. lemon juice
¼ tsp. seasoned salt
1 tbs. finely chopped
   parsley
⅓ cup chopped Hawaiian
   macadamia nuts or
   slivered almonds

Wipe fillets with damp cloth and sprinkle with salt. Roll and secure with toothpick. Place rolls in steamer or on wire rack above boiling water, cover and steam 15 mins. or until fish is opaque. Mix together onion, mayonnaise, lemon juice, seasoned salt and parsley. Carefully remove fillets from steamer and quickly spread each with mayonnaise mixture. Top each with nuts and serve immediately.

# MEATS & POULTRY

*Hawaiian Spareribs recipe calls for a variety of lush Pacific flavors.*

### SPARERIBS HAWAIIAN

2 lbs. lean spareribs
3 tbs. flour
1 tsp. salt
3 tbs. soy sauce
3 tbs. salad oil
2/3 cup sugar
2/3 cup wine vinegar

½ cup water
½ cup pineapple juice
1 tsp. grated fresh ginger
   root (or ½ tsp. dry ginger
2 cups fresh pineapple
   and papaya chunks

Cut spareribs into 2-inch pieces. Mix flour, salt and soy sauce together and coat ribs. Allow to stand 10 mins. Heat oil in skillet and brown ribs on all sides. Drain off excess fat and add sugar, vinegar, water, juice and ginger. Cover and simmer until meat is tender, about 45 mins. Stir in fruit and simmer 5 mins. longer. Serve garnished with minced parsley and sesame seeds.

## ISLAND SUKIYAKI

2 tsp. salad oil
1½ lbs. sirloin or tenderloin steak, sliced
  "bacon" thin, 2 inches
  long
¼ cup sugar
¾ cup soy sauce
¼ cup water, mushroom
  stock or white wine
2 med. onions, thin sliced
  lengthwise

1 green pepper, sliced
  thin
1 cup celery, sliced
  diagonally into ½-inch
  strips
1 12-oz. can bamboo
  shoots, sliced thin
1 cup fresh mushrooms
  (or canned) sliced thin
1 bunch green onions cut
  in 1-inch lengths

Heat oil in heavy skillet, add meat and brown lightly. Mix sugar, soy sauce and mushroom stock (water or wine) and add half this mixture to the meat. Stir and push meat to one side of pan and add onion, celery and pepper; cook a few minutes. Add remaining soy sauce liquid, bamboo shoots and mushrooms. Cook 3 to 5 mins. Add green onion tops and cook 1 minute more. Stir well and serve immediately with fluffy rice.

## KOWLOON GINGER BEEF WITH PAPAYA

1 fresh papaya
2 cups salted ice water
Few thin slices Spanish
  onion
1½ lbs. beef tenderloin,
  sliced paper thin
4 small pieces fresh
  ginger, sliced thin
½ tsp. salt

2 cups chicken broth
1 tsp. Chinese oyster sauce
  (purchased in Chinese
  grocery)
1 tsp. soy sauce
½ cup water
1 tsp. cornstarch
Peanut oil (for frying)

Peel the papaya, slice in small pieces or strips. Soak papaya slices in salted ice water for 1 hour. Rinse in cold water and drain. In skillet, sauté onion in oil until soft, add slices of beef, ginger and papaya, sauté for 2 to 3 minutes. Stirring carefully so as not to break the papaya slices. Add chicken broth and ½ tsp. salt, stirring carefully. Bring to boil. In saucepan mix the oyster sauce, soy sauce, water and cornstarch. Add to sautéed mixture and stir until thickened. Garnish with watercress. Serve with cooked rice.

## PINEAPPLE-BEEF TERIYAKI KEBABS

1½ lbs. sirloin or
    tenderloin steak
2 cups fresh pineapple,
    cut into 1-inch cubes
½ cup soy sauce
¼ cup brown sugar
½ tsp. salt

2 tbs. lemon juice
½ tsp. grated fresh ginger
    root (or ¼ tsp. dry
    ginger)
1 clove garlic, minced
1 tbs. salad oil

Cut meat into 1-inch pieces. Mix remaining ingredients and pour over meat and pineapple. Marinate at least 1 hour stirring twice. Thread   meat and pineapple on skewers alternately. Barbecue 2 to 4 inches from coals 5 to 10 mins. basting with marinade as each is turned. Serve with flower impaled on skewer after cooking.

## LANAI KEBABS

Alternate bits of fresh pineapple and ham on small skewers, brush with salad oil and charcoal broil until lightly browned.

## SWEET AND SOUR MEAT BALLS

1½ lbs. ground beef
2 eggs
4 tbs. corn starch
1 onion, minced
¼ tsp. pepper
¼ tsp. nutmeg
1 tsp. salt
¼ tsp. garlic powder or
    grated garlic
2 tbs. salad oil

1¼ cups pineapple juice
1 tbs. soy sauce
3 tbs. wine vinegar
⅓ cup water
½ cup brown sugar
2 cups fresh pineapple
    and papaya chunks
2 green peppers, cut
    bite-size

Blend together beef, eggs, 1 tsp. corn starch, onion, pepper, nutmeg, salt and garlic. Form into 1-inch balls. Heat oil in skillet and brown meat balls on all sides. In a large sauce pan, add remaining corn starch to pineapple juice along with soy sauce, vinegar, water and brown sugar. Cook until thickened stirring constantly. Add meat balls, fruit and green pepper and cook 5 mins., or until fruit is well heated. Serve sprinkled with chopped Hawaiian macadamia nuts or slivered almonds.

## BARBECUED HAM WIKI WIKI

2 medium ham slices,
  1-inch thick
1 tsp. sugar
1 tbs. dry mustard

¼ tsp. paprika
6 tbs. cider vinegar
2 to 4 tbs. guava jelly

Pan fry slices of ham on medium heat, remove and keep warm. To drippings add remaining ingredients, cook down and pour over ham and serve immediately. Garnish with sprigs of parsley or watercress.

## HAWAIIAN ROAST PORK WITH GUAVA JELLY GLAZE

5 to 6 lb. leg of pork
½ cup Hawaiian quava
  jelly

Pineapple slices
Maraschino cherries

Score surface of pork with sharp knife in 1-inch squares. Place in shallow roasting pan, scored side up and put in oven which has been pre-heated to 325°F. Roast for approximately 4½ hours, or until meat thermometer registers 185°F. One half hour before meat is done, remove from oven and coat with guava jelly. Return to oven and continue roasting until done. Garnish with glazed pineapple slices and cherries. Ring serving platter with parsley.

## SWEET ROAST PORK (Char Siu)

1½ lbs. boneless pork, cut
  1½-inches thick
3 tbs brown sugar
½ tbs. salt
¼ cup honey
1 tsp. soy sauce
1 tbs. white wine

3 tbs. nam yue (red bean
  curd sauce — may be
  omitted)
½ tsp. monosodium
  glutamate
1 tbs. red food coloring
⅓ cup water
⅛ tsp. heong liu fun (or
  allspice)

Cut pork into cubes and rub with sugar. Let stand for 5 mins. Combine remaining ingredients, pour over pork and marinate overnight in refrigerator. Drain pork and lay on rack placed over pan of water and roast at 350°F. for 1 hour. Turn after 30 mins. and baste with remaining sauce. Continue roasting for 30 mins. more. This roast is delicious served hot or cold when sliced ⅛-inch thick. It may be shredded and used as a topping for other dishes such as chop suey, chow mein, or fried rice.

## MOCK KALUA ROAST

2 5-lb. pork shoulder
   roasts (or fresh ham)
4 tbs. salad oil
1 garlic clove, minced

4 tbs. salt
Ti or banana leaves (corn
   husks or foil)

Mix the minced garlic with salad oil and rub roasts with mixture. Wrap meat in leaves, then in foil, securing seams tightly. Roast at 350° F. for four hours. Uncover meat and brown surface in hot oven, 450° F. or in broiler just before serving. Mock Kalua Roast should be cut into individual serving portions and eaten sprinkled with Hawaiian salt (or ice cream salt).

## PORK WITH NOODLES (Pansit)

1 pkg. fine noodles
1 tbs. shortening
1 clove garlic, crushed
1 small onion, sliced

1 lb. pork, cubed
½ lb. fresh shrimps
1 tsp. salt
dash of pepper

Cook noodles in a generous amount of boiling salted water until tender; drain. Heat shortening in skillet and add garlic. Cook for a few minutes; remove garlic and fry onion until partially cooked. Add pork and cook until meat is tender, adding the shrimps, salt and pepper when the pork is half cooked. Add noodles to pork and shrimp mixture and place on a large plate. Garnish with finely ground roasted peanuts or crisp fried bacon rind, slices of lemon, finely chopped onion, Chinese parsley (parsley), and strips of slightly beaten egg fried in tissue thin sheets.

## SPICED PORK CHOPS

6 pork chops, cut 1-inch
   thick
2 cloves garlic, minced
2 bay leaves
¾ cup wine vinegar

¾ cup water
1½ tsp. salt
2 peppercorns
2 tbs. shortening

Place all ingredients but shortening in a skillet and soak for 5 minutes. Cover, bring quickly to steaming and then lower heat and simmer until nearly dry. Add shortening and brown chops on both sides. Serve with vegetables such as cabbage or spinach. Just before serving toss the lightly cooked vegetable in frying pan after the chops have been removed. Additional vinegar may be added for flavor.

## CHINESE TOMATO BEEF

1 lb. lean beef, cut in
   thin slices
2 medium onions, cut in
   large pieces
1 green pepper, cut in
   large pieces

3 tomatoes, cut in wedges
5 tbs. peanut oil (or salad
   oil)
1 tbs. soy sauce
2 tsp. flour
1 clove garlic

Place the meat in a bowl and pour over a sauce made from 2 tbs. peanut oil, soy sauce and flour. Mix. Marinate for 20 mins., turning once. Heat 2 tbs. of the peanut oil in skillet and add garlic. Press garlic against sides of pan when browned and dry. Remove garlic and add the meat and marinade. Cook for 5 to 10 minutes, stirring frequently. Remove the meat and the gravy that has formed and set aside. Heat remaining peanut oil in skillet and add onions, green pepper and cook slightly. Add the meat, gravy and tomatoes. Heat until the gravy bubbles, remove and serve at once. Garnish with parsley or watercress.

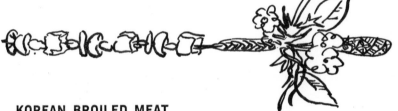

## KOREAN BROILED MEAT

3 lbs. lean beef (select
   round steak, short ribs,
   sirloin or similar cut)
Meat tenderizer
½ cup soy sauce
½ cup sesame oil (or
   salad oil)
¼ cup sugar

¼ tsp. salt
¼ tsp. black pepper
1 tsp. monosodium
   glutamate
2 cloves garlic, minced
3 green onions, chopped
2 tbs. sesame seeds,
   browned and crushed

If round steak or other boneless meat is used, cut into pieces about 3-inches square and about ⅓-inch thick. Pound the meat and score thoroughly, cutting in both directions. If short ribs are used remove bones and cut slices as directed above. Score thoroughly. Treat with tenderizer following directions on jar. Combine remaining ingredients and soak meat in this marinade for 1 hour or more. Drain meat and place on rack. Broil each side from 5 to 10 minutes or until brown, basting with marinade once on each side.

## HOW TO COOK KALUA PIG IN AN IMU (Hawaiian Pit Oven)

In a dry level spot of ground, dig a round pit large enough to hold a freshly dressed pig of at least 100 pounds. Next, select at least 80 to 100 dry and porous rocks about the size of your fist, and if they have not been heated before, heat them to red hot to prevent exploding during cooking. Cool rocks and keep dry. Line pit with gravel, additional rocks or fire bricks. Build a large fire in the center of the pit with wood shavings and split logs and lay rocks around the edges and within the fire so that they heat to red hot.

Meanwhile, prepare pig by cutting slits in the skin at neck and hind quarters. Rub plenty of Hawaiian salt or ice cream salt into these slits and throughout the inside cavity. Fill the cavity with hot rocks and tie closed with heavy cord. Tie all four feet together and wrap pig in chicken wire, securing all openings well.

Using a shovel, spread the remaining hot rocks out in the pit to form a depression to hold the pig. Line the depression with green banana, ti or other leaves and place pig in pit. Other items of food to be baked may also be added at this point, such as sweet potatoes, fish, chicken, lau laus, etc. Cover with additional leaves and wet burlap sacks. Shovel dry dirt over the entire pit, covering all traces of leaves and burlap. Seal edges well with dirt to prevent steam loss. Cook 4½ to 5 hours before uncovering.

Remove Kalua Pig and unwrap ceremonially. Cut into individual portions and serve as traditional Luau main course.

44

## MACADAMIA NUT TURKEY STUFFING

2 qts. bread crumbs
1 cup chopped onion
½ clove garlic, minced
½ cup celery, chopped
½ cup chopped celery
    leaves
½ cup butter or margarine
½ tsp. sage
½ tsp. thyme

½ tsp. crushed bay leaf
1½ tsp. salt
½ tsp. pepper
1 egg, beaten
1 tbs. brandy or sherry
    wine
1 cup Hawaiian macadamia
    nuts, chopped

Place bread cubes in a large bowl. Heat skillet, add butter.
Sauté onions, garlic, celery and celery leaves. Add to bread
cubes and combine with remaining ingredients. Toss together
lightly. If stuffing seems very dry, add melted butter, milk or
broth to moisten slightly. Stuff into salted turkey. Yield: 10 cups
of stuffing.

## WATERCRESS MEAT STIR

1 lb. lean pork or beef,
    cut in thin strips
1 tbs. crushed fresh ginger
    root (or ¼ tsp. ginger
    powder)
1 clove garlic, crushed
1 tsp. salt
1 lb. fresh watercress,
    washed

1 tbs. cornstarch
½ cup sugar
¼ tsp. monosodium
    glutamate
2 tsp. shoyu (soy sauce)
½ cup stock or water
Salad oil

Heat oil in skillet and brown meat with ginger and garlic. When
meat is well done, remove ginger and garlic. Season meat with
salt and pepper. Make a smooth paste by combining the cornstarch, sugar, monosodium glutamate, shoyu and water. Add
this paste to the cooked meat. When liquid comes to a boil,
add watercress stems, then leafy pieces. Cook until tender but
crisp (2 minutes).

## COCONUT CHICKEN

1½ cups coconut milk
(see recipe)
2 tbs. salad oil
2 frying chickens, meat
boned and cubed
1 tsp. seasoned salt
½ cup water

1 lb. fresh taro or spinach
leaves (1 pkg. frozen)
4 tbs. butter (or margarine)
½ tsp. monosodium
glutamate
1½ tsp. flour
3 cups mashed white
potatoes

Heat oil in skillet and sauté chicken cubes 10 mins. Add seasoned salt and water and cover, cooking 20 mins. over low heat. Wash and trim taro or spinach leaves. Melt butter (or margarine) in a sauce pan and add greens. Stir, cover and cook 10 mins. over low heat. Blend monosodium glutamate, flour and additional seasoned salt (if desired) to cooled coconut milk and add to chicken. Bring to boil, stirring occasionally to avoid sticking. Ring plates with hot mashed potatoes and spread a layer of greens in the center. Pour chicken mixture over top and garnish with paprika and chopped macadamia nuts. Or serve in individual casseroles or coconut shells.

## GAR DOO GAI (Chinese Chicken)

2½ lbs. chicken
Salt
Water
3 tbs. peanut oil (or
salad oil)
½ cup cooked long grain
rice

2 cups shredded lettuce
½ cup finely chopped
green onion
2 tbs. Chinese plum sauce
(or preserve)
½ cup Papaya Seed
Dressing (see recipe)

Season chicken with salt, cover with water and simmer until tender, about 1 to 1½ hours. Remove chicken from broth. When cool, remove meat from bones and cut into strips 1-inch long. Sauté chicken in 2 tbs. peanut oil until crisp. Remove chicken from skillet. Add remaining peanut oil to the skillet and heat until very hot. Add rice and fry, stirring constantly until hard and grainy, about 2 minutes. If skillet is not very hot, the rice will stick. Toss rice with lettuce, sautéed chicken, green onion, plum sauce and papaya seed dressing. Makes 5 to 6 servings.

## CHICKEN FRIED RICE

⅓ cup salad oil
4 cups cold cooked rice
1½ cups cold cooked
   chicken, slivered
1 green onion, chopped
¼ cup fresh mushrooms,
   sliced

2 eggs
1 tsp. soy sauce
½ tsp. monosodium
   glutamate
dash pepper

Heat oil in large skillet, add rice and stir until hot. Add chicken, onion, mushrooms and cook 5 minutes longer. Beat eggs with remaining ingredients and add to rice, stirring rapidly so that mixture blends with rice before setting. Serve oriental-style by pressing rice into a deep round bowl, then turning it out into a more shallow one to form a round top. Garnish with minced parsley or watercress and ring with bits of fresh papaya and pineapple.

## MAUI FRIED CHICKEN

3 fryer chickens
1 cup flour
2 tsp. salt
¾ tsp. black pepper
1½ cups pineapple chunks

1½ cups Coconut Milk
   (see recipe)
½ lb. butter or margarine
½ cup shredded coconut
Oil for frying

Cut fryers in half and dip in mixture of ½ cup flour, salt and pepper. Heat oil in a deep skillet and fry chicken to a golden brown color. Put chicken in baking pan and bake in oven at 350° F. till tender. In a sauce pan, heat coconut milk but do not boil. Mix butter and ½ cup flour in bowl. Add coconut milk gradually and whip until smooth. Add more coconut milk for desired thickness (not too thick). In skillet, sauté pineapple chunks in butter until lightly browned. Place chicken on serving platter, sprinkle with fresh shredded coconut. Serve with coconut sauce and sautéed pineapple in individual bowls. Serves 6.

## CHICKEN WITH TARO LEAVES

1 4-lb. chicken
3 tsp. salt

3 lbs. taro leaves (or
   spinach)
3 cups coconut milk,
   scalded

Cut chicken into small pieces. Put in large kettle, cover with hot water, add salt and simmer until tender. Wash taro leaves thoroughly; remove stem and fibrous part of veins. Put in covered sauce pan, add 1 cup water and cook for 15 mins. Drain and repeat twice more. (When substituting spinach for taro leaves, cook only once in salted water.) Pour coconut milk into drained taro leaves and gently stir. Place chicken in serving dish with 1 cup broth. Pour over taro mixture and serve.

## PINEAPPLE PEKING DUCK

**Pressed Duck:**
1 duck
salt

½ cup Chestnut flour
½ cup cracker meal

**Batter for deepfat frying pressed duck:**
1 cup flour
½ tsp. sugar
½ tsp. salt

1 egg
1 cup ice water
2 tbs. peanut oil (or salad oil)

**Pineapple Sweet-Sour Sauce:**
1 cup pineapple juice
1 cup fresh pineapple chunks
½ cup vinegar
1 6-oz. can tomato paste
¾ cup sugar
1 cup water

1 tsp. salt
½ fresh green pepper, cut in large pieces
½ small onion, cut in large pieces
2 tbs. cornstarch
½ cup water
Sesame seeds

Season duck with salt, steam for about 1½ hours. When duck is tender, remove bones. Place boned duck in shallow greased loaf pan and press until flat. Cover both sides of duck with mixture of chestnut flour and cracker meal, sprinkle lightly with water. Steam until flour is cooked and browned, about ½ hour. Remove molded pressed duck from pan and cool. Cut duck into strips. Dip strips in batter for deepfat frying. Fry strips in hot peanut oil until crisp. Drain on absorbent paper. Keep warm. Combine sweet-sour sauce ingredients, except sesame seeds in saucepan and bring to boil stirring constantly. When thickened, pour sauce over duck, sprinkle with sesame seeds and serve immediately. Serves 6.

# THE COLORFUL FOODS OF HAWAII

*Lush tropical fruits, nuts and seafood present a beautiful complement to Hawaii's attractive people and landscape, as pictured from the Reef Hotel, Waikiki Beach.*

Vanda orchids are used to garnish a variety of "pupus" or Hawaiian appetizers. As served at the Tahitian Lanai Restaurant, Waikiki Beach to Hula accompaniment.

# HAOLE LUAU MENU
### (as pictured)

**Ambrosia Polynesian**            **Pineapple-Sweet Potato Islandia**

**Hawaiian Fruit Boat**

**Lomi Salmon**            **Hawaiian Roast Pork With Guava Jelly Glaze**

Pictured against vast pineapple field near Wahiawa, Oahu, is an attractive way to prepare and serve fresh pineapple cubes in "boats." A ripe pineapple will feel like the inside of your wrist when thumped with a finger.

Fresh Hawaiian pineapple dishes at right are, from top, Tropical Fruit Plate, Fresh Pineapple Frappe, Pineapple Chicken Salad, Minted Pineapple Cup, Fresh Pineapple Wedge and Tropical Fruit Freeze.

Hawaiian papayas offer a versatility in serving and cutting which is unique. Peeling is best done with a potato peeler to preserve most of the fruit. Scoop out seeds with a teaspoon. Slices may be cut lengthwise and arranged in fan shape. Round slices lend themselves to garnishes. Notched treatment of papaya halves make a beautiful salad or dessert. Papayas may also be cubed and added to many meat or fruit dishes to create an exotic flavor. They are equally delicious cooked or eaten fresh.

An Island version of Shrimp Salad is served in papaya with mayonnaise or sour cream.

Orchids lend a touch of tropical elegance to a variety of ways to prepare fresh pineapple salads.

# ISLAND LUAU MENU
*(as pictured)*

| | |
|---|---|
| Spareribs Hawaiian | Chicken Fried Rice |
| Lomi Salmon | |
| Macadamia Nuts | Diamond Head Sweets |
| Coconut Chicken | |
| Tahitian Poi | Fresh Papaya Slices |
| Haupia        (not pictured) | Luau Punch |

# Decorations and Entertaining...

A festive Hawaiian atmosphere can be accomplished by decorating both the luau table and dining area with as many green leaves and flowers as can be obtained. Ferns, palm or banana leaves are best. Grass matting can transform large areas into tropical backgrounds. Fresh fruit, such as pineapple, papaya and banana can be used in colorful arrangements. Fresh flowers should be used in abundance for garnishing both foods and settings, and to be strung on threads to provide each guest with a "lei" or Hawaiian garland. Sea shells and nets also provide decor. A decorative IPUHAOLE PUNCH BOWL can serve as centerpiece and is made by hollowing out a large watermelon. Be sure to have the Hawaiian music playing in the background — maybe someone knows the hula!

# ORIENTAL LUAU MENU
### (as pictured)

Won Ton (Crab Puffs)      Green Salad with Papaya Seed Dressing

Holiday Sweet Bread

Tempura Shrimp                    Pineapple Peking Duck

Spareribs Hawaiian

Oriental Egg Rolls                       Fresh Tropical Fruit

*Pork chops are a favorite Hawaiian entree and are comple-
mented by rice, fresh papaya and cottage cheese. Papaya
Melba dessert is in center.*

Imagination and color distinguish Hawaiian beverage favorites as pictured at Fisherman's Wharf Restaurant, Honolulu.

Savor the exotic flavors of the orient by marinating steaks with Teriyaki Sauce (see recipe) and serve with grilled pineapple.

The blue Pacific waters around Hawaii abound with a variety of colorful fish and seafood. A traditional Island favorite is Grilled Mahi Mahi, pictured at Hilo Bay, Hawaii. Fisherman in background practices ancient art of net throwing.

PHOTOGRAPHY CREDITS

The Editorial Staff and Publisher of the Pacifica House HAWAII Cook Book wish to thank the Fruit Shippers of Hawaii (Henderson Associates, Inc.) for furnishing many photographs reproduced on these pages and on the cover.

Individual photographs are by:
Don Jim, pages 51 (and cover), 53, 54, 55, 58, 60, 62, 64.
Don FitzGerald, pages 49, 50, 52, 56 & 57, 61, 63.

Ice cream and sherbet with the delicate flavor of papaya create festive Hawaiian desserts.

Hawaiian Fruit Boat salad can be turned into a hot weather surprise by topping with scoops of ice cream or sherbet.

Fresh Hawaiian papayas are becoming a mainland favorite, thanks to jet-air freight. Papayas are seen growing in the lava beds near Hilo, Hawaii.

A classic finish to any Hawaiian menu is yours with Papaya ala Meringue and Sweet Leilani's Crown desserts, pictured on the next page with fresh fruits and Papaya Seed Dressing.

## POLYNESIAN BAKED CHICKEN

2 frying chickens, cut up
1 cup flour
1½ tsp. seasoned salt
½ lb. butter (or margarine)
1 cup orange juice

2 tbs. lemon juice
½ cup brown sugar
1 tbs. corn starch
1 tbs. soy sauce
1 fresh pineapple, cubed
1 fresh papaya, cubed

Shake chicken parts in paper bag with flour and seasoned salt. Melt butter (or margarine) and rub 2 tbs. of it into a large baking dish. Place in chicken and brush remaining butter over each piece. Bake 50 mins. at 350°F. or until chicken is browned. Meanwhile, combine juices, sugar, soy sauce, and corn starch in a sauce pan and bring to a boil, stirring constantly. Remove from heat when clear and thickened and add fruit. Pour mixture over chicken, coating each piece, and bake 10 mins. longer. Serve garnished with chopped parsley or green pepper and sesame seeds.

## CHICKEN POT ROAST

3 lbs. chicken thighs and
   drumsticks
½ tsp. salt
¼ cup soy sauce
2 tbs. salad oil
1 tbs. grated fresh ginger
   root (or ½ tsp. ground
   ginger)
1 tbs. sherry wine
1 cup fresh mushrooms
   (or canned)

½ cup Chinese peas (or
   tender green beans)
2 green onions, cut in
   1-inch pieces
1 tbs. cornstarch
1 cup water
1 tbs. soy sauce
1 tsp. monosodium
   glutamate
1 tsp. brown sugar

Rub chicken pieces with salt and the ¼ cup soy sauce, let stand 15 mins. Heat oil in skillet and brown chicken well on all sides. Combine ginger and sherry, pour over chicken; cover and simmer for 30 minutes or until chicken is tender. Add mushrooms the last 5 minutes of cooking. Transfer chicken to serving dish and keep warm. Leave mushrooms in skillet, add vegetables and remaining ingredients, cook until sauce thickens stirring occasionally. Pour over chicken and serve.

# VEGETABLES & FRUITS

*Typical Hawaiian vegetables are, from left, packaged poi, taro root, bean sprouts, China peas, water chestnuts, fresh ginger root, mushrooms, white (daikon) radish.*

## BAKED TARO

Wash fresh taro root well, trim and peel. Bake at 400°F. from 1 to 1½ hours, or until tender. Break open much like a baked potato, or cut into serving portions and season with salt, pepper and butter.

## CHINA PEAS WITH MUSHROOMS

| | |
|---|---|
| 1½ lbs. China Peas (Snow peas) | ½ lb. fresh mushrooms |
| 1 onion, sliced | 2 tbs. salad oil |
| | 2 tbs. soy sauce |

Wash China Peas and pull away stems. Rinse mushrooms and, if large, cut into halves or quarters. Drop peas into 2 cups boiling water, stir and cover. Simmer 5 minutes, drain. Meanwhile, heat oil in skillet and sauté onions and mushrooms 5 minutes. Add peas and soy sauce, stir and cook 1 minute longer. Do not overcook — peas should be slightly crisp. Serve immediately.

## GUAVA GLAZED SWEET POTATOES

8 medium sweet potatoes,
  cooked and peeled

1 cup guava jelly
2 tbs. butter or margarine

Arrange sweet potatoes in a single layer in oiled baking dish. In saucepan, heat jelly and butter to form syrup. Drizzle one-half of jelly mixture over potatoes and bake in oven at 350°F. for about 15 minutes. Carefully turn potatoes and add remaining syrup. Bake 15 minutes more, basting potatoes occasionally, if necessary to obtain perfect glaze.

## LUAU SWEET POTATO CASSEROLE

6 cups mashed cooked
  sweet potatoes
3 cups crushed pineapple
2 tsp. seasoned salt

½ lb. butter (or margarine)
¾ cup brown sugar
¼ tsp. nutmeg

Melt butter (or margarine) and combine with all ingredients except nutmeg. Spread into casserole and sprinkle on nutmeg. Bake 45 mins. at 375°F. Serve in individual cups or large shells.

## PAN FRIED TARO

Prepare Baked Taro (see recipe) or boil peeled fresh taro root until tender, about 1 hour. Slice into ⅜-inch slices. Heat oil or butter in a skillet and brown taro slices lightly on both sides. Serve hot, much as you would hash browned potatoes for breakfast, or as vegetable course with any meal.

## PINEAPPLE-SWEET POTATO ISLANDIA

6 medium sweet potatoes,
  cooked until just tender
  — peeled
½ large pineapple, peeled
  and cut in wedges
¼ cup butter or
  margarine

¾ cup brown sugar,
  packed
½ cup water
½ tsp. salt
¼ tsp. monosodium
  glutamate

Arrange halved sweet potatoes and pineapple wedges alternatively in well greased baking dish. Combine remaining ingredients in skillet and simmer 5 minutes. Pour mixture over sweet potatoes and pineapple, bake at 400°F. for 20 to 25 minutes, turning occasionally to glaze properly.

## GREEN BEANS AND PORK

1 cup pork slices
3 tbs. shoyu (soy sauce)
½ tsp. garlic powder
1 tsp. sesame seeds

1 medium onion
2 pkgs. thawed French
  cut beans
Bacon fat

Melt 1 tbs. bacon fat in skillet over medium heat. Add pork cut in strips 2-inches long by ¼-inch thick. Cook until pork is white. Add garlic powder, shoyu and seeds. Cut onion in half across diameter. Place cut side down and slice in ¼-inch slices. Add onion to pork and cook for 10 minutes, stirring often. Add drained beans, cook and stir 10 minutes. Medium heat should be used throughout cooking. Add no extra liquid.

## CURRY STUFFED AVOCADO

Blend 2 cups cooked cubed lamb, seafood or chicken with Hawaiian Curry Sauce (see recipe) and spoon into avocado halves. Broil or bake until tops are browned. Serve with chutney and fresh chopped pineapple and papaya garnish.

## DIAMOND HEAD SWEETS

Drain canned sweet potatoes (or peeled cooked sweet potatoes or yams) and brush with melted butter (or margarine) and sprinkle with brown sugar. Bake 20 mins. at 350°F. or until slightly browned. Serve on ti or other green leaf.

## PACIFIC ASPARAGUS

1½ lbs. fresh asparagus
2 tbs. butter or
  margarine
¼ cup water

½ tsp. seasoned salt
¼ tsp. monosodium
  glutamate
1 tsp. soy sauce

Cut tender portion of asparagus diagonally to bite-size and rinse. Melt butter (or margarine) in skillet, add water, seasoned salt, monosodium glutamate and soy sauce. When mixture boils, add asparagus, toss lightly and cover. Cook 2 to 3 mins. over medium-high heat. Serve with macadamia nut garnish.

## GINGERED CARROTS

3 to 5 medium-size carrots
½ cup water
½ tsp. monosodium
  glutamate

1 tsp. grated ginger root
1 tsp. sugar
2 tbs. butter or margarine

Peel carrots. Cut into strips, add water and monosodium gultamate. Simmer over low heat for about 10 minutes or till tender. Add ginger, sugar and butter. Cook for about 2 to 3 minutes longer, turning carrots carefully several times. Serve hot garnished with parsley.


## COCONUT MILK SPINACH

2 pkgs. frozen spinach
1 cup coconut milk
1 tsp. salt

¼ tsp. monosodium
  glutamate

Cook spinach as directed on package until tender. Drain and place in serving dish. Pour on the coconut milk which has been heated slowly just to the boiling point. If desired, add 1 to 2 tsp. prepared horseradish to the coconut milk just before serving.

## MACADAMIA NUT STUFFED EGGPLANT

3 medium eggplants
1 tsp. salt
¼ tsp. monosodium
  glutamate
Dash of pepper
1½ tsp. sugar
1 onion, chopped

3 tbs. butter
2 tbs. catsup
1 tsp. Worcestershire sauce
2 eggs, beaten
2/3 cup chopped Hawaiian
  macadamia nuts
⅓ cup buttered crumbs

Cut washed eggplants in half lengthwise and cook for 15 minutes in boiling water. Drain and scoop out the centers when cool, leaving a shell about ¼-inch thick. Chop the pulp and cook in salted water until tender, drain. Add seasonings to the pulp. Sauté onions in butter and add to pulp. Mix all remaining ingredients except the crumbs and add to pulp. Scoop filling into eggplant shells, sprinkle top of each with crumbs and place in oiled baking dish. Bake in oven at 375°F. for 25 minutes. Serve with tomato sauce.

## LANAI BAKED BEANS

3 cans New England-style beans (tomatoless)
1 fresh pineapple, cubed
¼ cup pineapple or orange juice
¼ cup brown sugar
1 cup cubed cooked ham (bacon, beef or pork may be used)
1 tsp. dry mustard
1 tsp. salt
2 tbs. butter (or margarine)

Rub deep casserole with butter (or margarine) and pour in beans. Blend brown sugar, mustard and salt with juice and stir into beans along with half the pineapple and half the meat. Arrange remaining fruit and meat atop mixture and bake 1 hr. at 350°F. Cover casserole during last 20 mins. if fruit browns too fast.

## WATERCRESS BEAN SPROUT NAMASU

1 bunch watercress
1 8-oz. pkg. fresh bean sprouts
1 tsp. sesame seeds, toasted and crushed
¼ cup vinegar (or 3 tbs.
vinegar and 1 tbs. lemon juice)
¼ cup sugar
¼ tsp. salt
⅛ tsp. monosodium glutamate

Wash watercress and cut into 1-inch lengths. Wash and cook bean sprouts in boiling water for about 2 minutes, drain. Combine remaining ingredients, except sesame seeds, and pour over watercress and bean sprouts that have been mixed gently together. Serve garnished with sesame seeds.

## JAPANESE SWEET PICKLES

2 lbs. Diakon (white Japanese radish)
1 cup sugar
¼ cup white vinegar
1 cup water
3 tbs. salt
3 drops yellow food coloring

Wash daikon and peel; slice very thin. Combine remaining ingredients in a sauce pan and bring to a boil. Place daikon slices in 2-quart jar and pour over hot liquid. Cool to room temperature and cover. Refrigerate at least 3 days before serving.

## AMBROSIA POLYNESIAN

2 cans mandarin oranges,
  drained
2 bananas

¾ cup flaked coconut
12 maraschino cherries
½ cup pineapple juice

Slice bananas and dip into juice of mandarin oranges (this keeps them from turning dark). Combine all ingredients and chill for at least 2 hours. Just before serving, toss lightly to blend fruit.


## FRESH PAPAYA WITH LIME JUICE

Peel papaya with potato peeler. Cut in half and scoop out seeds (save seeds for Papaya Seed Dressing). Slice lengthwise or cut in cubes. Sprinkle liberally with fresh lime juice and chill for at least 30 minutes before serving.

## MINTED PINEAPPLE CUP

Fresh pineapple — cubed,
  ¾ cup per serving

Fresh mint sprigs
2 tsp. sugar per serving

Crush 4 mint leaves per serving in bowl. Add sugar. Mix and add fresh pineapple. Chill thoroughly. Serve in sherbet glasses which have been chilled.


## FRESH LIME-BANANA COCKTAIL

Juice of 2 fresh limes
½ cup catsup
3 tbs. celery, finely
  chopped
Dash of onion salt
¼ tsp. monosodium
  glutamate

¼ tsp. curry powder
2 tsp. Worcestershire sauce
3 cups bananas, sliced in
  rounds (just before
  serving)

Blend together all ingredients except bananas and chill. Gently fold in banana rounds and serve on lettuce leaves or in cocktail glass.

## ISLAND PAPAYA COCKTAIL

Juice of 2 limes
3 cups papaya, diced or
   balls
1 tbs. sugar

1 tbs. butter
3 tbs. mayonnaise
1 tbs. catsup
1 tsp. grated onion

Marinate papaya for 30 minutes in lime juice in refrigerator. Carmelize sugar in saucepan. Combine the remaining ingredients except papaya and lime juice, and gradually add to sugar. Cook mixture over low heat until well blended. Place chilled papaya in cocktail glasses and top with a spoonful of cooled sauce. Garnish with a few of the papaya seeds and serve.

## PAPAYA FRUIT PLATE HAWAIIAN

Color, flavor and texture contrasts are extremely important in arranging fresh fruit plates. For a truly interesting combination, arrange alternating rows of sliced papaya, pineapple wedges, and wedges of watermelon on a colorful platter. Garnish with fresh strawberries and mint leaves to simulate strawberry leaves. Serve well chilled with hot rolls and iced tea for a light luncheon.

## PAN FRIED PAPAYA

Peel papaya and cut into ½ inch slices or thinner. Sprinkle with lemon or lime juice and allow to stand for 10 minutes. Fry in butter or margarine until just lightly browned on the outside, the center still firm. Serve as entree with meat or seafood dishes or as an attractive and tasty garnish.

## HAWAIIAN FRUIT FRITTERS

2 eggs
¼ cup milk
½ tsp. salt
2 cups fresh pineapple,
   papaya, banana or mango

2 cups finely crushed corn
   flakes
1½ cups salad oil

Beat eggs, milk and salt together. Cut fruit into inch-long pieces and dip in egg mixture and roll in crumbs. Deep fry in oil until golden brown.

## TAHITIAN POI

Pure Hawaiian poi, a pasty staple made from the Taro root, often is too startling a taste for "Haoles" (mainlanders). In Tahiti, the natives blend their poi half and half with mashed bananas. The flavor is most delightful. Use fresh or canned poi, available at supermarkets. This blend also may be eaten with the fingers, Hawaiian style, and is a must on all Luau menus!

## FRESH PINEAPPLE PICKLES

| | |
|---|---|
| 1 fresh pineapple (4 to 6 cups) | Dash of salt |
| 2 cups sugar | 1 cup vinegar |
| 2 cups water | 1 stick cinnamon |
| | 2 to 4 whole cloves |

Peel pineapple and cut crosswise into 1-inch thick slices. Remove core and cut into sections about 1-inch wide. Mix sugar and water in saucepan; add pineapple pieces and boil for about 10 minutes. Remove pineapple. To the syrup, add vinegar and spices. Boil until syrup is thickened. Add pineapple back into syrup and boil for about 5 minutes. Pour into hot sterilized jars and seal.

## FRESH PINEAPPLE CHUTNEY

| | |
|---|---|
| 1 medium pineapple (4 cups chopped) | 2 tbs. finely chopped garlic (5 cloves) |
| 1½ cups white vinegar | 3 Hawaiian red peppers, seeded and finely chopped (small red hot chilies) |
| 1½ cups brown sugar | |
| 1 15-oz. pkg. raisins | |
| 1 tbs. salt | 1 cup chopped Hawaiian macadamia nuts (or almonds) |
| 2 tbs. finely chopped ginger root (1 tsp. ground ginger) | |

Peel and core pineapple, cut into small pieces. Combine with all other ingredients except nuts. Cook slowly until pineapple is tender (about 30 mins.). Add nuts and cook until chutney is of desired consistency. Stir frequently to prevent scorching. Pour into sterilized jars and seal. Yield: 4 pints.

## KIM CHEE (Oriental Relish)

1 medium head of cabbage (or 1 lb. chopped celery)
½ cup salt
4 cups water
1 tsp. crushed dry red pepper
1 clove garlic, finely minced

½ tsp. chopped ginger root (or dash of dry ground ginger)
2 tsp. chopped green onions
1 tsp. monosodium glutamate
½ tsp. salt
1½ tsp. sugar

Wash cabbage and shred fine. Add ½ cup salt and 4 cups of water, soak for 1 hour. (When using chopped celery eliminate this step). Drain and rinse cabbage well. Add red pepper, garlic, ginger, green onions, and remaining ingredients. Press down into a jar, cover and refrigerate for at least 2 days for relish to "ripen." Serve with Oriental meat dishes.

## FRESH GINGER ROOT

The smooth-skinned and bumpy root native to India and cultivated in all tropical countries and in Hawaii. Prized for its strong piquant aroma and sweet peppery flavor, ginger root is used primarily as a condiment. Store in cool dry place. Uses: Peeled and unpeeled ginger is popular in making chutney, fruit preserves, marinades, baked goods and sauces. Use it grated, chopped or whole, rubbed on meats and seafood. (1 part dry ginger equals 4 parts fresh, though not really interchangeable.)

## WATER CHESTNUTS

Slice canned and peeled water chestnuts in thin slices so that they may be alternated with other ingredients for a change in texture — a really crisp taste treat but one which never dominates.

## FRESH WATER CHESTNUTS

The nut-like fruit of an aquatic plant, it is a basic ingredient in all Chinese cooking and Chop Suey. Brown outside and white inside, water chestnuts are noted for their fresh crispness. Add them to favorite vegetable recipes, salads and meat stew dishes. Keep refrigerated. Uses: Peel the day of purchase and boil 15 minutes in plain water. May be stored for weeks refrigerated if water is changed every three days. Slice and add to recipes shortly before serving; they need only be heated.

# Oriental Vegetable Cookery Tips:

## PANNED VEGETABLES

Select fresh leafy green vegetables such as Swiss chard, spinach, white or green mustard, cabbage or celery cabbage. Wash thoroughly and trim, discarding inedible parts. Shake free of as much water as possible. Cut heavy lower stems into pieces and slice upper leaves into sections. For each quart of vegetables, melt one tablespoon of shortening (bacon fat, butter, margarine or oil) in a sauce pan. Add vegetables, placing stems on the bottom and the leaves on the top. Sprinkle salt through the vegetables. Cover and cook 5 to 7 minutes or until just tender. Stir by shaking the pan without removing the lid.

## "STIR-FRIED" VEGETABLES

Vegetables such as sliced celery, China peas, green pepper pieces, bean sprouts, cauliflower, broccoli, onion, or tomato quarters are often stir-fried. They are cooked in a small amount of oil, at a very high temperature, with continuous stirring until just barely tender. To shorten the time for stir-frying, some vegetables such as cauliflower may be blanched for 2 or 3 minutes before frying.

## SECRETS OF ORIENTAL VEGETABLE COOKERY

To vary the flavor of either panned, stir-fried or steamed vegetables, add a small amount of sake (Japanese rice wine) or soy sauce.

Sliced water chestnuts, mushrooms, slivered toasted almonds, chopped macadamia nuts, or toasted and crushed sesame seeds may be blended with or sprinkled on top of the vegetable for added flavor or contrast in texture.

Cook vegetables such as broccoli, green beans, asparagus, zucchini, and cabbages until they are just barely tender. Watch them carefully as it is better to undercook than to overcook. They must retain their crispness.

Vegetables such as carrots, celery, green beans and broccoli are often sliced diagonally to improve the appearance and to gain tenderness in spite of the brief cooking period. Do not, however, cut any vegetable so fine that it looses its identity — with the possible exception of onion and garlic.

# BREAD & DESSERTS

*Fresh Papaya-Nut Pie is made from lush Hawaiian fresh papayas.*

## HOLIDAY SWEET BREAD (Pao Doce)

3 tbs. sugar
2 pkgs. active dry yeast
½ cup lukewarm potato
    water
1 cup mashed potatoes
⅛ tsp. ginger
½ cup milk

2 tsp. salt
6 eggs
1¾ cups sugar
½ cup melted butter or
    margarine
8 cups flour

Add the sugar and yeast to potato water, stir until dissolved.
Blend in potatoes and ginger. Set aside to rise until doubled
in bulk. Scald milk, add salt and cool to luke warm. Beat eggs;
add sugar gradually while continuing to beat; stir in cooled
butter. Combine yeast and egg mixtures; blend thoroughly. Stir
in 2 cups of flour, add milk and beat until thoroughly blended.
Add 2 more cups of flour; beat 5 minutes. Add remaining flour

gradually, kneading when dough becomes too stiff to beat. Turn out on a floured board and knead 10 mins. adding only enough extra flour to prevent sticking. Place dough in an oiled bowl, cover and let rise in warm place until doubled in bulk. Divide dough into 4 portions; shape into round loaves on oiled cookie sheets or place in oiled loaf pans. Allow to rise until doubled in bulk. Brush loaves with beaten egg; bake at 350°F. for 50 mins. or until brown.

## BANANA MUFFINS

1¾ lbs. ripe bananas
¾ lb. butter or margarine
3 cups sugar
6 eggs, well beaten
⅛ tsp. banana extract

⅛ tsp. vanilla extract
4 cups cake flour
½ tsp. salt
1¾ tbs. baking soda

Cream butter and sugar, add eggs, bananas and extracts in mixing bowl. Stir well. Add flour, salt and baking soda, which has been sifted 3 times. Do not overmix. Pour into well oiled muffin pans and bake in oven at 350°F. for 30 to 40 minutes.

## BANANA - NUT BREAD

2 cups flour, sifted
¾ cup sugar
3 tsp. baking powder
1 tsp. salt
½ tsp. soda
½ tsp. cinnamon

1 cup chopped Hawaiian
   macadamia nuts (or
   almonds, walnuts)
1 egg, beaten
1 cup mashed bananas
2 tbs. shortening, melted

Sift all dry ingredients together. In separate bowl, beat egg, stir in bananas and shortening. Stir into dry ingredients, just enough to blend, add nuts. Pour into greased loaf pan (8 x 4 x 4-inches), and bake in a moderate oven — 350°F. for 1 hour. Cool on rack.

## PINEAPPLE BRAN MUFFINS

1 egg
2 tbs. melted shortening
¾ cup crushed pineapple
1¼ cup flour
6 tbs. sugar

1½ tsp. baking powder
¼ tsp. soda
¾ tsp. salt
½ cup bran flakes
⅓ cup chopped walnuts

Beat the egg, add the melted shortening and undrained pineapple. Sift together dry ingredients and stir into the pineapple mixture. Add the bran flakes and the nuts. Pour into well oiled muffin pans and bake in oven at 375°F. for 30 minutes. Yield: 12 muffins.

## GUAVA MUFFINS

1 cup milk
2 eggs, beaten
2 cups flour
3 tbs. sugar

½ tsp. salt
1 tbs. baking powder
3 tbs. melted shortening
½ cup cooked guava pulp

In mixing bowl, add milk to eggs and stir. Sift together dry in-gredients and add to egg mixture. Stir in shortening and guava pulp, mxing only until blended. Fill oiled muffin pans about 2/3 full. Bake at 400°F. for 20 minutes. Remove from pan im-mediately.

## POI MUFFINS

1⅓ cups flour
½ tsp. salt
1 tbs. sugar
4 tsp. baking powder

2/3 cup poi
1 egg
3 tbs. melted butter or
  margarine

Sift dry ingredients together. Use poi as purchased, do not mix with water. Blend poi with remaining ingredients and add to dry ingredients. Stir only until thoroughly mixed. Spoon oiled muffin pans 2/3 full and bake at 400°F. for 30 minutes. If fresh poi is not obtainable, use ⅓ cup of milk mixed with the canned poi.

## TROPICAL FRUIT BRAN MUFFINS

1 egg
2 tbs. butter (or margarine)
¾ cup crushed fresh
  papaya or pineapple
  (or mixture of both)
1¼ cups flour

6 tbs. sugar
1½ tbs. baking powder
¼ tsp. soda
¾ tsp. salt
½ cup bran flakes

Beat egg, add melted butter and fruit pulp. Sift together dry ingredients and stir into fruit mixture, then add bran. Rub muffin pans with additional butter and fill ¾ full. Bake 30 mins. at 375°F.

## PAPAYA OATMEAL SQUARES

1 cup flour
½ tsp. salt
½ tsp. soda
½ cup brown sugar, firmly
   packed
⅓ cup butter or margarine
1 cup rolled oats

Papaya Filling:
1 cup diced ripe papaya
⅓ cup sugar
2 tsp. fresh lime juice
½ cup chopped Hawaiian
   macadamia nuts (or
   almonds)

Sift together first three ingredients. Add brown sugar. Cut in butter until mixture is consistency of cornmeal. Add rolled oats and mix well. Press half of mixture into oiled 6 x 11-inch pan. Combine papaya, sugar, lime juice and nuts and spread over crumb mixture. Sprinkle remaining crumb mixture over fruit layer and press evenly with hands. Bake in oven at 350°F. for 40 minutes. Cool in pan. Cut in small squares, rectangles or triangles, according to personal preference.

## COCONUT UPSIDE DOWN CAKE

½ cup butter or margarine
1½ cups grated fresh
   coconut

1 cup brown sugar

Melt butter and sugar in an 8-inch square cake pan. Sprinkle coconut over the mixture and spread to an even thickness. Prepare cake batter as follows:

¼ cup shortening
½ cup sugar
1 egg
1 cup cake flour
1½ tsp. baking powder

⅛ tsp. salt
⅓ cup milk
½ tsp. vanilla extract
Whipped cream

Cream shortening and sugar. Add egg and beat thoroughly. Sift dry ingredients together and add alternately with combined milk and vanilla to the creamed mixture. Pour over the coconut and bake in oven at 350°F. for 45 minutes. Remove from pan immediately. Serve topped with whipped cream.

## COCONUT CANDY

1½ cups sugar
½ cup water
2 tsp. light corn syrup

1½ cups grated fresh
coconut

Combine sugar, water and corn syrup in sauce pan. Boil until it spins a thread 2-inches long (248°F.). Remove crystals from the sides of the pan with a pastry brush dipped in water. Remove syrup from heat, stir in the coconut. Boil in mixture until very thick (236°F.) and again remove from heat. Beat until it becomes creamy and is of the proper consistency to drop from a spoon on waxed paper. If desired, 4 tbs. of drained crushed pineapple may be added to the syrup with the coconut. Yield: 2 dozen pieces.

## MOLOKAI FRUIT SQUARES

12-oz. pkg. crushed vanilla
wafers
¼ lb. butter (or margarine)
softened
½ cup chopped Hawaiian
macadamia nuts (or
cashews)

1 cup fresh papaya chunks
1 cup fresh pineapple
chunks
½ cup pineapple syrup
(or cane syrup)

Combine all ingredients except syrup and pack in shallow cake pan. Chill thoroughly several hours. Cut in 2-inch squares and serve topped with syrup and a spot of whipped cream.

## PAPAYA ALA MERINGUE

3 egg whites
½ tsp. vinegar
¼ tsp. almond extract
Dash salt

1 cup sugar
1 large papaya
Juice of ½ lime

Combine egg whites, vinegar, almond extract and salt in mixing bowl, beat until mixture forms stiff peaks. Add sugar gradually and continue beating until very stiff. Line cookie sheet with plain ungreased paper. Divide meringue into six mounds on paper and form into cups with spoon. Bake in slow oven, 300°F. for 45 minutes. Remove from paper immediately and cool. Peel papaya with potato peeler, cut in half and scoop out seeds. Cut into bite-size cubes or make into balls. Squeeze over lime juice, chill. Just before serving, fill meringue shells with papaya, a dollop of almond flavored whipped cream may be added.

## FRESH PINEAPPLE-NUT BREAD

1¾ cups sifted flour
2 tsp. baking powder
½ tsp. salt
¼ tsp. soda
¾ cup coarsely chopped
  Hawaiian macadamia
  nuts
¾ cup brown sugar,
  firmly packed

3 tbs. soft butter or
  margarine
2 eggs
1 cup finely chopped fresh
  pineapple (packed firmly
  so cup is filled with
  juice and pineapple bits)
Topping:
2 tbs. sugar
½ tsp. cinnamon

Sift together first four ingredients. Add nuts to dry ingredients. Cream together sugar, butter and eggs until fluffy. Stir in half the flour mixture. Add pineapple. Blend in remaining flour mixture and pour into well greased 9 x 5 x 3-inch pan. Combine topping ingredients and sprinkle over top of bread mixture. Bake in 350°F. oven for about 1 hour.

## COCONUT WAFFLES HAWAIIAN

2 cups sifted all-purpose
  flour
1 tsp. salt
1 tsp. baking soda
1 tsp. baking powder
2 cups buttermilk

4 eggs
2/3 cup melted butter or
  margarine
½ cup shredded or flaked
  coconut

Sift together dry ingredients. Beat eggs until light. Add dry ingredients and buttermilk alternately to eggs, beginning and ending wih dry ingredients. Add melted butter and coconut, blend thoroughly. Makes 8 waffles. Serve waffles piping hot, topped with slices or rounds of fresh papaya which has been lightly sprinkled with fresh lime or lemon juice. Dribble coconut syrup over waffles and papayas — enjoy with a bit of Hawaiian relaxation!

## HAWAIIAN FRUIT CREPES

Thin standard hotcake batter to the consistency of cream with cold water. Beat in 1 egg and 2 tbs. flour. In a medium hot small greased skillet, pour in about 3 tbs. batter (for a single crepe) and tilt pan so that batter flows to cover entire bottom of pan. Turn as soon as batter sets and cook 30 seconds longer. Remove crepe and repeat procedure for each crepe required (1 per serving). In a sauce pan, heat 2 cups crushed pineapple, or a blend of fresh cubed pineapple, papaya and banana, and season with cinnamon, brown sugar and rum (optional) to taste. Spoon mixture generously onto each crepe and roll up. Serve hot, topped with sour cream or whipped cream, and dots of Hawaiian jam or jelly.

## HAUPIA (COCONUT PUDDING)

**3 tbs. corn starch**
**3 tbs. sugar**
**⅛ tsp. salt**

**2 cups Coconut Milk (see recipe)**

Combine dry ingredients. Add ½ cup of the coconut milk and blend to a smooth paste. Heat the remaining milk on low heat; add corn starch mixture, stirring constantly and cook until smooth and thickened. Pour into a shallow pan; let cool until firm. Cut into six squares and serve on small plates or pieces of ti leaf as Luau dessert.

## MANGO TAPIOCA PUDDING

**2½ cups mango slices**
**canned**
**2 cups mango juice**
**1 tbs. lemon juice**

**¼ cup sugar**
**¼ cup minute tapioca**
**1 tbs. butter or margarine**

Drain mango slices and save juice. Arrange slices in a buttered baking dish. Over the top pour mango juice which has been mixed with lemon juice, sugar and tapioca. Dot with butter. Bake covered at 350°F. for 45 minutes. Fresh mangoes may be used. Cut slices from ripe mangoes. Add water to partially cover the remaining pits and cook 10 minutes. Squeeze pulp from pits and use with juice.

# FRESH PAPAYA-NUT PIE OR TARTS

1 cup orange juice
2 tbs. corn starch
¼ cup sugar
1½ cups sliced fresh papaya

1 tbs. lemon juice
½ cup chopped Hawaiian
    macadamia nuts
Whipped cream

Pre-bake a pie shell using Flake Pie Crust recipe. Blend orange
juice with corn starch, add sugar and lemon juice. Heat slowly
in sauce pan, stirring constantly, until clear and thickened.
Place sliced papaya in pie shell and pour over juice mixture.
Cool to room temperature, then chill. Serve ringed with whipped
cream and sprinkled with chopped Hawaiian macadamia nuts,
almonds or cashews. For Tarts, pre-bake shells in muffin pans
and fill with papaya mixture.


# BANANA HONEYS

8 ripe bananas
Juice of 1 lemon
2 tbs. butter or margarine
1 cup honey

1¼ cups coconut cream
    (see recipe)
1 cup grated fresh coconut

Peel and cut bananas in 1½-inch pieces and place in a shallow
oiled baking dish. Add lemon juice and dot with butter. Pour
honey over all. Bake in oven at 400°F. for 20 minutes. Serve
hot with coconut cream and grated fresh coconut. Serves 6.


# PINEAPPLE WIKI WIKI DESSERT

2 cups canned unsweet-
    ened pineapple juice
2 tbs. lemon juice
1½ cups sugar
1 tsp. salt
2 tbs. unflavored gelatin

½ cup cold water
6 egg yolks, well beaten
6 egg whites, stiffly beaten
1 cup heavy cream,
    whipped
3 dozen ladyfingers

Combine pineapple juice, lemon juice, sugar, and salt in a
saucepan. Heat, stirring occasionally, until sugar is dissolved.
Remove from heat. Soften gelatin in cold water and dissolve
into hot mixture. Gradually stir into the egg yolks. Chill until
partially set. Fold in egg whites and whipped cream. Line bottom and sides of a well oiled 9-inch spring form pan with ladyfingers. Pour in the filling and chill until firm. Garnish with
additional whipped cream and well drained crushed pineapple
if desired.

## PASSION FRUIT CHIFFON CAKE

2¼ cups cake flour
1 cup sugar
1 tsp. salt
1 tbs. baking powder
½ cup salad oil
5 egg yolks
½ cup water

¼ cup frozen passion
   fruit juice, thawed (or
   frozen pineapple juice)
1 cup egg whites
½ tsp. cream of tartar
⅓ cup sugar

Sift flour, the 1 cup of sugar, salt and baking powder into mixing bowl. Make a well in the flour mixture and add oil, egg yolks, water and juice. Beat with a spoon until smooth. Beat egg whites with cream of tartar until whites form soft peaks. Add the ⅓ cup of sugar gradually beating after each addition. Beat until meringue is just stiff enough not to slide when bowl is inverted. Gradually pour yolk mixture over meringue, gently folding with rubber spatula until just blended. Pour into unoiled 10-inch tube cake pan. Bake in oven at 325°F. for 1 hour. Immediately turn pan upside down on cake rack and let hang until cold. Remove the cake from pan. Frost with Passion Fruit 7 Minute Frosting (see recipe).

## PASSION FRUIT 7-MINUTE FROSTING

2 egg whites
1½ cups sugar
⅛ tsp. salt

6 tbs. frozen passion fruit
   juice, thawed (or frozen
   pineapple juice)
2 tsp. light corn syrup

Combine all ingredients in saucepan. Beat over low heat with a rotary beater until sugar is dissolved. Cook for 7 minutes, beating constantly, or until frosting will stand in peaks. Remove from the heat, beat until thick enough to spread.

## FLAKE PIE CRUST

1¾ cups flour
1 tsp. salt

1½ cubes butter (or
   margarine)
⅓ cup ice water

Sift flour and salt into mixing bowl and cut in butter using two table knives, one in each hand, until mixture is in pea-size bits. Sprinkle in water a tablespoon at a time, stirring with fork until dough forms a ball (all water may not be required). Wrap in wax paper and chill before rolling out for best results.

## HAWAIIAN BANANA PIE

4 cups sliced bananas,
   ripe but firm
½ cup pineapple juice
½ cup sugar

1 tsp. cinnamon
1 tbs. butter (or margarine)
Pastry for 2 crust pie

Soak sliced bananas in pineapple juice for 20 to 30 mins. Drain saving the juice. Place bananas in pastry lined pie plate, add sugar and cinnamon which have been mixed together. Add 2 tbs. of the pineapple juice. Dot with butter and cover with top crust. Bake at 400°F. for 30 to 45 minutes, or until crust is browned.


## HAWAIIAN MACADAMIA NUT PIE

4 eggs, slightly beaten
¾ cup sugar
1½ cups light corn syrup
¼ tsp. salt

1½ cups Hawaiian
   macadamia nuts,
   chopped coarsely
1½ tsp. vanilla
1 unbaked pie shell

Combine egg, sugar, syrup, nuts, salt and vanilla. Pour into unbaked pie shell and bake at 350°F. for about 10 minutes. Reduce temperature to 325°F. and bake 30 minutes more. Ring with whipped cream before serving.


## PASSION FRUIT CHIFFON PIE

4 eggs, separated
1 cup sugar
½ tsp. salt
½ cup frozen passion
   fruit juice, thawed (or
   frozen pineapple juice)

1 tbs. unflavored gelatin
¼ cup cold water
1 tsp. grated lemon rind
1 baked pie shell
½ cup heavy cream,
   whipped

Beat egg yolks until thick. Add ½ cup of sugar, salt and juice. Cook over low heat until thick, stirring constantly. Add gelatin which has been softened in the cold water, stirring until gelatin is dissolved. Add lemon rind and cool until slightly congealed, fold in stiffly beaten egg whites to which the remaining ½ cup sugar has been added. Pour into baked pie shell and chill until firm. Ring with whipped cream. A sprinkling of chopped Hawaiian macadamia nuts may be added before serving.

## CHINESE ALMOND COOKIES

½ lb. butter (or margarine)
2½ cups sifted flour
½ tsp. baking soda
½ tsp. salt

1 cup sugar
1 egg, slightly beaten
2 tsp. almond extract
50 blanched almonds

Cut butter (or margarine) into sifted dry ingredients. Add egg and extract and blend well. Shape into 1-inch balls and place on ungreased cookie sheet. Flatten cookies and press one almond into the center of each. Bake 12 to 15 mins. at 350°F. Turn out on wire screen to cool. Yield: 5 dozen.

## MACADAMIA NUT TEA COOKIES

1 cup soft butter or
   margarine
½ cup sifted confectioners'
   sugar
1 tsp. vanilla

2½ cups sifted flour
¼ tsp. salt
¾ cup finely chopped
   Hawaiian macadamia
   nuts

In bowl, mix the butter, sugar and vanilla together thoroughly. Sift flour and salt together and stir into butter mixture. Add nuts and mix well. Roll into 1-inch balls. Place on ungreased baking sheet. Bake at 400°F. until set but not brown, about 10 to 12 minutes. While still warm, roll in confectioners' sugar. Cool. Roll in sugar again.

## OATMEAL BANANA COOKIES

¾ cup shortening
1 cup sugar
1 egg
1 cup mashed bananas
1 cup rolled oats
½ cup chopped Hawaiian
   macadamia nuts

1½ cups flour
½ tsp. soda
1 tsp. salt
¼ tsp. nutmeg
¾ tsp. cinnamon

Cream shortening and sugar. Add egg and beat thoroughly. Mix in bananas, rolled oats and nuts. Sift together remaining ingredients and add to the banana mixture. Drop by teaspoonfuls on an oiled cookie sheet about 1½ inches apart. Bake at 400°F. for about 12 minutes. Yield: 3½ dozen tropical flavored cookies.

## SWEET LEILANI'S CROWN

**1 pkg. orange gelatin**         **1 pkg. lime gelatin**
**1 large papaya**

Prepare orange gelatin according to directions on package, chill until thick but not set. Peel papaya and remove seeds. With melon baller, make enough papaya balls to fill ring salad mold with one papaya ball in each indentation. Pour orange gelatin into mold, place remaining papaya balls (if any), into gelatin, chill until firm. Prepare lime gelatin and chill until thick. Mash remaining papaya pulp. Whip lime gelatin until frothy, add papaya pulp. Pour mixture over orange gelatin which is firmly set. Return to refrigerator and chill until firm. Unmold and serve with Chinese Almond Cookies (see recipe).

## TROPICAL FRUIT FREEZE

Cut top from fresh pineapple for each serving and scoop out center. Dice a portion of the removed pineapple and blend with diced papaya. Spoon mixture into shell to about half full and top with lime sherbet. Garnish with cherry. Place in freezer until solid (at least 6 hours). Remove from freezer a few minutes before serving to allow frost to form on outside of pineapple shell.

## AVOCADO SHERBET

1⅛ cups sugar
1½ cups water
¾ cup lemon juice

Grated rind of 1 lemon
1½ cups avocado pulp

Boil sugar and water together for 5 minutes. Add lemon juice and lemon rind to the avocado pulp. Then slowly add cooked sugar syrup. Blend thoroughly. Pour into refrigerator tray and freeze with temperature set to coldest. Stir once during freezing.

## FRESH PINEAPPLE FRAPPE

1 cup fresh pineapple
    cubed

2 tbs. honey
1 pint vanilla ice cream

Place all ingredients in the order listed in blender. Mix at top speed only till the pineapple and ice cream are blended. Pour into small goblets or juice glasses, top with chopped fresh pineapple and serve immediately. Serves 4.

## PAPAYA FRUIT ICE

1 can frozen orange juice,
    thawed
2 ripe papayas, peeled
    and diced
4 ripe bananas, diced

1 can water (using orange
    juice can)
Juice of 1 lemon (or lime)
1 cup sugar

Combine all ingredients in blender and blend until smooth. Pour into freezing trays and freeze until firm, stirring or blending once during freezing. Served garnished with Hawaiian macadamia nuts.

## SNOWBALL SUNDAE WITH RUM PINEAPPLE

1 14-oz. jar papaya-
    pineapple jam
6 tbs. dark rum

Vanilla ice cream
Shredded Coconut, toasted

Simmer jam in saucepan for 10 minutes stirring frequently. Cool and add rum. Roll ice cream balls in coconut, serve topped with rum pineapple sauce. Top with chopped Hawaiian macadamia nuts if desired.

*Beautifully garnished Hawaiian drinks are pictured at Tahitian Lanai Restaurant.*

## BANANA COW

| | |
|---|---|
| 1 jigger light rum | 3 oz. milk |
| Dash of Angostura Bitters | ½ ripe banana |
| Dash of vanilla extract | Shaved ice |
| ½ oz. of simple syrup | Nutmeg |

Blend all ingredients except nutmeg, in electric blender. Pour into cocktail glass, top with sprinkling of nutmeg (optional). This exotic drink may also be served without liquor.

## PAPAYA MILK SHAKE

| | |
|---|---|
| 2 large ripe papayas | 3 cups milk |
| 2/3 cup sugar | 1 tsp. nutmeg |
| ¼ cup lemon or lime juice | 1 cup cracked ice |

Peel papayas with potato peeler, remove seeds and mash with fork. Combine all ingredients but nutmeg in blender or shake in jar. Serve topped with nutmeg.

## BOO LOO (Chinese for pineapple)

| | |
|---|---|
| 1 Hawaiian pineapple | 2 jiggers pineapple juice |
| 1 jigger Demarara rum | 1 jigger fresh lime juice |
| 1 jigger amber rum | 1 jigger honey |
| ½ jigger 150 proof dark rum | 1 jigger soda water |
| ½ jigger Jamaica rum | Few chunks fresh pineapple |

Hollow the center of the fresh pineapple, leaving about one inch of fruit in the shell. Cut the pineapple top at a slant. Put all the ingredients in a blender and blend well. Pour into hollowed pineapple, add a long straw, replace pineapple top before serving.

## HAWAIIAN OKOLEHAO COCKTAILS

Okolehao, Hawaii's original liquor distilled from the root of the ti plant, can be adapted to most favorite cocktail recipes. About 80 proof, Okolehao resembles a light brandy, bourbon or Scotch. Substitute this native Hawaiian favorite in recipes for fizzes, collins, old fashions, mixed drinks and with soda. Okolehao is favored by many throughout the Pacific just "on the rocks."

## PINO PEPE

| | |
|---|---|
| 1 jigger light rum | ¼ oz. lemon juice |
| 1 jigger vodka | Juice of fresh lime (save |
| Dash of Triple Sec. Liquor | shell for garnish) |
| Dash of Rock Candy Syrup | Shaved ice |
| 2 oz. pineapple juice | |

Blend all ingredients together in electric blender. Pour into shell of fresh pineapple or tall glass. Garnish with pineapple spear topped with maraschino cherry.

## MAI - TAI

| | |
|---|---|
| Shaved ice | 2½ oz. light rum |
| Juice of one lime | ½ oz. dark rum |
| ½ tsp. simple syrup | Sprig of mint |
| ½ tsp. Orange Curacao | Pineapple spear |

Fill a 14-ounce glass with shaved ice. Stir in lime juice, syrup, Curacao and light rum. Drop in half of lime shell. Float dark rum on top. Garnish with a pineapple spear topped with sprig of mint. Float vanda orchid for a really regal touch. Serve with straws. For added festive touch, use pineapple shell (cut top off and scoop out pineapple) as serving mug.

## HAWAIIAN SAKE & SAKE MARTINI

An excellent Hawaiian sake (same as the traditional Japanese rice wine) is made in Honolulu, by more than one fine sake brewery. It is imported to the mainland and available throughout the islands. Especially good as a Luau beverage, either hot or cold, Hawaiian sake also is excellent served "on the rocks" with a lemon twist.

Substitute Hawaiian sake (or Japanese sake) for gin or vodka in your favorite martini recipe. Garnish with usual olive or onion, or with Japanese Sweet Pickle (see recipe) and top pick with a vanda orchid or small flower.

## TROPICAL TEA PUNCH (for 50)

4 cups boiling water
1 cup tea leaves
4 cups sugar
4 cups cold water
12 cups pineapple juice

2 cups tart juice (guava, lemon, lime, or passion fruit)
Block of ice

Add boiling water to tea leaves and steep for 5 minutes. Strain, add sugar, stirring until dissolved. Cool mixture. Stir in remaining ingredients and chill. Serve Tropical Tea in punch bowl with block of ice. Float washed vanda orchids for true tropical effect. Makes about 6 quarts, or 50 half-cup servings.

## PEARL HARBOR (NAVY) GROG

1 oz. fresh lime juice
1 oz. fresh orange juice
1 oz. fresh pineapple juice
1 oz. passion fruit nectar

⅓ jigger light rum
1⅓ jiggers dark rum
½ cup finely cracked ice

Pour juices into blender then add rums and mix for 20 seconds. Pour unstrained into a large Old Fashioned glass half-filled with finely cracked ice. Garnish with mint sprigs and serve with straws.

## VANDA DAIQUIRI

1½ jiggers light rum
½ jigger dark rum
   (Jamaica)
Dash of Rock Candy Syrup
   or simple syrup

1 oz. pineapple juice
½ oz. lemon juice
Shaved ice

Blend all ingredients together in electric blender. Serve in large saucer type glass, float Vanda Orchid on top.

## ISLAND SUNRISE COCKTAIL

1 can papaya juice
1 can guava juice

1 can pineapple juice

Blend and chill juices. Stir well before serving with a sprig of mint or watercress.

## LUAU PUNCH

1 can (46-oz.) pineapple
   juice
1 can guava nectar

1 can papaya nectar
1 qt. ginger ale
1 qt. mint or lime sherbet

Freeze opened cans of juice just past the mushy stage. Pour it and the ginger ale over sherbet in a punch bowl. Yield: 1 gallon.

## POI COCKTAIL

1 cup prepared poi
1 cup vanilla ice cream
⅓ cup sugar

2 cups milk
¼ cup sherry wine
dash of nutmeg

Whip poi, ice cream, and sugar until smooth. Add milk gradually, beating continually. Blend in the wine and serve with nutmeg sprinkled over the surface.

## PAPAYA ONO ONO COCKTAIL

4 cups ripe papaya pulp
1 cup passion fruit juice
   or nectar
¼ cup lemon or lime juice
2½ cups guava juice or
   nectar

½ cup orange juice
¾ cup sugar
4 cups unsweetened
   pineapple juice
½ cup cold water
Crushed ice

Blend papaya pulp, sugar and water in electric blender for 2 minutes. Add remaining ingredients, mix well and chill. Serve in tall glass over crushed ice (optional), garnish with sprig of mint and maraschino cherry. If crushed ice is used, serve with straws.

## PINEAPPLE MINT ICED TEA

½ cup tea leaves
10 cups boiling water
Sprigs of fresh mint
2 cups sugar

2 cups water
Juice of 5 lemons
Ice cubes
Pineapple spears

Pour boiling water over tea leaves and steep 3 to 5 minutes. Strain and add 4 mint sprigs, allow to cool. Remove mint. While cooling, simmer sugar and water together to form syrup. Combine tea and syrup, chill thoroughly. Add lemon juice. Pour over ice cubes in tall glass. Garnish with pineapple spear topped with fresh mint sprig. Yields: 3 quarts of refreshing beverage.

ALOHA NUI

# INDEX TO RECIPES

# The Hawaiian Language

The Hawaiian Language is musical and easy to learn! It is rich in descriptive terms. There are 12 letters in the alphabet . . . five Latin vowels — seven consonants. The vowels are pronounced as ah, ay, ee, o, oo. The consonants are h, k, l, m, n, p, and w. Every word and every syllable ends with a vowel and two consonants can never occur without a vowel between them. Some words have triple vowel formations and each vowel must be pronounced distinctively and separately.

# Popularly Used Hawaiian Words:

Akamai—clever
Aikane—friend
Aku—bonito fish
Alani—orange
Aloha—love, affection, welcome, greeting, goodbye
Aloha Nui Nui—especially big "aloha'
Aole—no
Haole—foreigner
Hauoli—Makahiki Hou—"happy new year"
Halakahiki—pineapple
Hale—house
Hana—work
Hanau—happy birthday
Hapa—half
Hapa haole—half foreigner
Hapia—carry
Hikiee—large couch
Holoku—long dress with train
Hoolaulea—festive gathering
Hui—club, organization
Hukilau—net fishing festival
I'a—fish
I'a maka—raw fish
Imu—underground oven
Ipo—sweetheart
Ipu pu—squash
Ipuhaole—watermelon
Kai—salt water
Kala—money
Kalua—to bake underground
Kamaaina—oldtimer, resident
Kane—male, husband
Kanaka—man
Kaola—broiled
Kapahaki—cooked
Kapu—forbidden, keep out
Kaukau—food, meals
Keiki—child
Ki—tea
Ko paa—sugar
Kope—coffee
Laiki—rice
Lanai—porch, patio
Lei—flower necklace

Limu—sea weed
Lomi—rub, knead
Luau—feast, leaves of taro
Mahalo—thanks, admire
Mahalo Nui—many thanks
Maia—banana
Maikai—good, wholesome
Malihini—tourist, stranger
Malolo—flying fish
Manauahi—extra, free
Mele Kalikimaka—Merry Christmas
Mele—song
Moa—chicken
Muumuu—loose fitting dress
Nani—beautiful
Nioi—pepper
Niu—coconut
Nui—big, great
Okole Maluna—bottoms up (toast)
Onaona—lovely
Ono Ono—delicious
Okolehao—ti root liquor
Opae—shrimp
Opihi—shellfish
Opu—abdomen
Paa Kai—salt
Pali—cliff, peak
Papale—hat
Pa-u—grass skirt
Pau—finished
Pelehu—turkey
Pipikaula—beef jerky
Poi—pasty staple food from taro root
Pua—flower
Pupu—appetizer
Uala—sweet potato
Ula—lobster
Wahine—female
Wai—water, liquid
Waiu—milk
Waiupaa—cheese
Waina—grapes, wine
Wela—hot
Wela Kahao—whoopy, hot time
Wikiwiki—quick, hurry up